AMERICAN FOREIGN POLICY

Three Essays

HENRY A. KISSINGER

AMERICAN FOREIGN POLICY

Three Essays

W · W · NORTON & COMPANY · INC · *New York*

77271

CONTENTS

Three THE VIETNAM NEGOTIATIONS

PREFACE

THE ESSAYS brought together in this volume approach questions of foreign policy from somewhat different angles. In "Domestic Structure and Foreign Policy" I consider the difficulties introduced into the conduct of international affairs in a world composed of nations with widely different social and political systems. In the second essay, "Issues of American Foreign Policy," I focus particularly on the need for developing a new concept of international order based on political multipolarity in a world in which two powers possess overwhelming military strength. Finally, in "The Vietnam Negotiations," my concern is with the peace negotiations on Vietnam: the lessons that have been learned from the proceedings and the advantages of first seeking agreement among the contending parties on ultimate goals and then working back to details that will implement them. All these essays were written before I took leave from the faculty of Harvard.

"Domestic Structure and Foreign Policy" first appeared in the Spring 1966 issue of *Daedalus* (Vol. 95, No. 2, of the Proceedings of the American Academy of Arts and Sciences); "Central Issues of American Foreign Policy" was a contribution to *Agenda for the Nation* (Washington, D.C.: The Brookings Institution, 1968); and "The Vietnam Negotiations" was published in the January 1969 issue of *Foreign Affairs* (Vol. 47, No. 2). I am grateful to these publications for giving me the opportunity to gather the essays into a single volume.

Henry A. Kissinger

Washington
January 1969

ONE

DOMESTIC STRUCTURE AND FOREIGN POLICY

I. THE ROLE OF
DOMESTIC STRUCTURE

IN THE traditional conception, international relations are conducted by political units treated almost as personalities. The domestic structure is taken as given; foreign policy begins where domestic policy ends.

But this approach is appropriate only to stable periods because then the various components of the international system generally have similar conceptions of the "rules of the game." If the domestic structures are based on commensurable notions of what is just, a consensus about permissible aims and methods of foreign policy develops. If domestic structures are reasonably stable, temptations to use an adventurous foreign policy to achieve domestic cohesion are at a minimum. In these conditions, leaders will generally apply the same criteria and hold similar views about what constitutes a "reasonable" demand. This does not guarantee agreement, but it provides the condition for a meaningful dialogue, that is, it sets the stage for traditional diplomacy.

When the domestic structures are based on fundamentally different conceptions of what is just, the conduct of international affairs grows more complex. Then it becomes difficult even to define the nature of disagreement because what seems most obvious to one side appears most problematic to the other. A policy dilemma arises because the pros and cons of a given course seem evenly balanced. The definition of what constitutes a problem and what criteria are relevant in "solving" it reflects to a considerable extent the domestic notions of what is just, the pressures produced by the decision-making process, and the experience which forms the leaders in their rise to eminence. When domestic structures—and the concept of legitimacy on which they are based—differ widely, statesmen can still meet, but their ability to persuade has been reduced for they no longer speak the same language.

This can occur even when no universal claims are made. Incompatible domestic structures can passively generate a gulf, simply because of the difficulty of achieving a consensus about the nature of "reasonable" aims and methods. But when one or more states claim universal applicability for their particular structure, schisms grow deep indeed. In that event, the domestic structure becomes not only an obstacle to understanding but one of the principal issues in international affairs. Its requirements condition the conception of alternatives; survival seems involved in every dispute. The symbolic aspect of foreign policy begins to overshadow the substantive component. It becomes difficult to consider a dispute "on its merits" because the disagreement seems finally to turn not on a specific issue but on a set of values as expressed in domestic arrangements. The consequences of such a state of affairs were explained by Edmund Burke during the French Revolution:

I never thought we could make peace with the system; because it was not for the sake of an object we pursued in rivalry with each other, but with the system itself that we were at war. As I understood the matter, we were at war not with its conduct but with its existence; convinced that its existence and its hostility were the same.[1]

Of course, the domestic structure is not irrelevant in any historical period. At a minimum, it determines the amount of the total social effort which can be devoted to foreign policy. The wars of the kings who governed by divine right were limited because feudal rulers, bound by customary law, could not levy income taxes or conscript their subjects. The French Revolution, which based its policy on a doctrine of popular will, mobilized resources on a truly national scale for the first time. This was one of the principal reasons for the startling successes of French arms against a hostile Europe which possessed greater over-all power. The ideological regimes of the twentieth century have utilized a still larger share of the national effort. This has enabled them to hold their own against an environment possessing far superior resources.

Aside from the allocation of resources, the domestic structure crucially affects the way the actions of other states are interpreted. To some extent, of course, every society finds itself in an environment not of its own making and has some of the main lines of its foreign policy imposed on it. Indeed, the pressure of the environment can grow so strong that it permits only one interpretation of its significance; Prussia in the eighteenth century and Israel in the contemporary period may have found themselves in this position.

But for the majority of states the margin of decision has been greater. The actual choice has been determined to a considerable degree by their interpretation of the environment and by their leaders' conception of alternatives. Napoleon rejected peace offers beyond the dreams of the kings who had ruled France by "divine right" because he was convinced

1. Edmund Burke, *Works* (London, 1826), Vol. VIII, pp. 214–215.

that *any* settlement which demonstrated the limitations of his power was tantamount to his downfall. That Russia seeks to surround itself with a belt of friendly states in Eastern Europe is a product of geography and history. That it is attempting to do so by imposing a domestic structure based on a particular ideology is a result of conceptions supplied by its domestic structure.

The domestic structure is decisive finally in the elaboration of positive goals. The most difficult, indeed tragic, aspect of foreign policy is how to deal with the problem of conjecture. When the scope for action is greatest, knowledge on which to base such action is small or ambiguous. When knowledge becomes available, the ability to affect events is usually at a minimum. In 1936, no one could know whether Hitler was a misunderstood nationalist or a maniac. By the time certainty was achieved, it had to be paid for with millions of lives.

The conjectural element of foreign policy—the need to gear actions to an assessment that cannot be proved true when it is made—is never more crucial than in a revolutionary period. Then, the old order is obviously disintegrating while the shape of its replacement is highly uncertain. Everything depends, therefore, on some conception of the future. But varying domestic structures can easily produce different assessments of the significance of existing trends and, more importantly, clashing criteria for resolving these differences. This is the dilemma of our time.

Problems are novel; their scale is vast; their nature is often abstract and always psychological. In the past, international relations were confined to a limited geographic area. The various continents pursued their relations essentially in isolation from each other. Until the eighteenth century, other continents impinged on Europe only sporadically and for relatively brief periods. And when Europe extended its sway over much of the world, foreign policy became limited to the Western Powers with the single exception of Japan. The international system of the nineteenth century was to all practical purposes identical with the concert of Europe.

The period after World War II marks the first era of truly global foreign policy. Each major state is capable of producing consequences in every part of the globe by a direct application of its power or because ideas can be transmitted almost instantaneously or because ideological rivalry gives vast symbolic significance even to issues which are minor in geopolitical terms. The mere act of adjusting perspectives to so huge a scale would produce major dislocations. This problem is compounded by the emergence of so many new states. Since 1945, the number of participants in the international system has nearly doubled. In previous periods the addition of even one or two new states tended to lead to decades of instability until a new equilibrium was established and accepted. The emergence of scores of new states has magnified this difficulty many times over.

These upheavals would be challenge enough, but they are overshadowed by the risks posed by modern technology. Peace is maintained through the threat of mutual destruction based on weapons for which there has been no operational experience. Deterrence—the policy of preventing an action by confronting the opponent with risks he is unwilling to run—depends in the first instance on psychological criteria. What the potential aggressor believes is more crucial than what is objectively true. Deterrence occurs above all in the minds of men.

To achieve an international consensus on the significance of these developments would be a major task even if domestic structures were comparable. It becomes especially difficult when domestic structures differ widely and when universal claims are made on behalf of them. A systematic assessment of the impact of domestic structure on the conduct of international affairs would have to treat such factors as historical traditions, social values, and the economic system. But this would far transcend the scope of this essay. For the purposes of this discussion we shall confine ourselves to sketching the impact of two factors only: administrative structure and the formative experience of leadership groups.

II. THE IMPACT OF THE
ADMINISTRATIVE STRUCTURE

In the contemporary period, the very nature of the governmental structure introduces an element of rigidity which operates more or less independently of the convictions of statesmen or the ideology which they represent. Issues are too complex and relevant facts too manifold to be dealt with on the basis of personal intuition. An institutionalization of decision-making is an inevitable by-product of the risks of international affairs in the nuclear age. Moreover, almost every modern state is dedicated to some theory of "planning"—the attempt to structure the future by understanding and, if necessary, manipulating the environment. Planning involves a quest for predictability and, above all, for "objectivity." There is a deliberate effort to reduce the relevant elements of a problem to a standard of average performance. The vast bureaucratic mechanisms that emerge develop a momentum and a vested interest of their own. As they grow more complex, their internal standards of operation are not necessarily commensurable with those of other countries or even with other bureaucratic structures in the same country. There is a trend toward autarky. A paradoxical consequence may be that increased control over the domestic environment is purchased at the price of loss of flexibility in international affairs.

The purpose of bureaucracy is to devise a standard operating procedure which can cope effectively with most problems. A bureaucracy is efficient if the matters which it handles routinely are, in fact, the most frequent and if its procedures are relevant to their solution. If those criteria are met, the energies of the top leadership are freed to deal creatively with the unexpected occurrence or with the need for innovation. Bureaucracy becomes an obstacle when what it defines as routine does not address the most significant range of issues or when its prescribed mode of action proves irrelevant to the problem.

When this occurs, the bureaucracy absorbs the energies of top executives in reconciling what is expected with what happens; the analysis of where one is overwhelms the consideration of where one should be going. Serving the machine becomes a more absorbing occupation than defining its purpose. Success consists in moving the administrative machine to the point of decision, leaving relatively little energy for analyzing the merit of this decision. The quest for "objectivity"— while desirable theoretically—involves the danger that means and ends are confused, that an average standard of performance is exalted as the only valid one. Attention tends to be diverted from the act of choice—which is the ultimate test of statesmanship—to the accumulation of facts. Decisions can be avoided until a crisis brooks no further delay, until the events themselves have removed the element of ambiguity. But at that point the scope for constructive action is at a minimum. Certainty is purchased at the cost of creativity.

Something like this seems to be characteristic of modern bureaucratic states whatever their ideology. In societies with a pragmatic tradition, such as the United States, there develops a greater concern with an analysis of where one is than where one is going. What passes for planning is frequently the projection of the familiar into the future. In societies based on ideology, doctrine is institutionalized and exegesis takes the place of innovation. Creativity must make so many concessions to orthodoxy that it may exhaust itself in doctrinal adaptations. In short, the accumulation of knowledge of the bureaucracy and the impersonality of its method of arriving at decisions can be achieved at a high price. Decision-making can grow so complex that the process of producing a bureaucratic consensus may overshadow the purpose of the effort.

While all thoughtful administrators would grant in the abstract that these dangers exist, they find it difficult to act on their knowledge. Lip service is paid to planning; indeed planning staffs proliferate. However, they suffer from two debilities. The "operating" elements may not take the planning effort seriously. Plans become esoteric exercises which are accepted largely because they imply no practical consequence. They are a sop to administrative theory. At the same time, since planning staffs have a high incentive to try to be "useful," there is a bias against novel conceptions which are difficult to adapt to an administrative mold. It is one thing to assign an individual or a group the task of looking ahead; this is a far cry from providing an environment which encourages an understanding for deeper historical, sociological, and economic trends. The need to provide a memorandum may outweigh the imperatives of creative thought. The quest for objectivity creates a temptation to see in the future an updated version of the present. Yet true innovation is bound to run counter to prevailing standards. The dilemma of modern bureaucracy is that while every creative act is lonely, not every lonely act is creative. Formal criteria are little help in solving this problem because the unique cannot be expressed "objectively."

The rigidity in the policies of the technologically advanced societies is in no small part due to the complexity of decision-making. Crucial problems may—and frequently do—go unrecognized for a long time. But once the decision-making apparatus has disgorged a policy, it becomes very difficult to change it. The alternative to the status quo is the prospect of repeating the whole anguishing process of arriving at decisions. This explains to some extent the curious phenomenon that decisions taken with enormous doubt and perhaps with a close division become practically sacrosanct once adopted. The whole administrative machinery swings behind their implementation as if activity could still all doubts.

Moreover, the reputation, indeed the political survival, of most leaders depends on their ability to realize their goals, however these may have been arrived at. Whether these goals are desirable is relatively less crucial. The time span by which administrative success is measured is considerably shorter than that by which historical achievement is determined. In heavily bureaucratized societies all pressures emphasize the first of these accomplishments.

Then, too, the staffs on which modern executives come to depend develop a momentum of their own. What starts out as an aid to decision-makers often turns into a practically autonomous organization whose internal problems structure and sometimes compound the issues which it was originally designed to solve. The decision-maker will always be aware of the morale of his staff. Though he has the authority, he cannot overrule it too frequently without impairing its efficiency; and he may, in any event, lack the knowledge to do so. Placating the staff then becomes a major preoccupation of the executive. A form of administrative democracy results, in which a decision often reflects an attainable consensus rather than substantive conviction (or at least the two imperceptibly merge). The internal requirements of the bureaucracy may come to predominate over the purposes which it was intended to serve. This is probably even more true in highly institutionalized Communist states—such as the U.S.S.R.—than in the United States.

When the administrative machine grows very elaborate, the various levels of the decision-making process are separated by chasms which are obscured from the outside world by the complexity of the apparatus. Research often becomes a means to buy time and to assuage consciences. Studying a problem can turn into an escape from coming to grips with it. In the process, the gap between the technical competence of research staffs and what hard-pressed political leaders are capable of absorbing widens constantly. This heightens the insecurity of the executive and may thus compound either rigidity or arbitrariness or both. In many fields—strategy being a prime example—decision-makers may find it difficult to give as many hours to a problem as the expert has had years to study it. The ultimate decision often depends less on knowledge than on the ability to brief the top administrator —to present the facts in such a way that they can be absorbed rapidly. The effectiveness of briefing, however, puts a premium on theatrical qualities. Not everything that sounds plausible is correct, and many things which are correct may not sound plausible when they are first presented; and a second hearing is rare. The stage aspect of briefing may leave the decision-maker with a gnawing feeling of having been taken —even, and perhaps especially, when he does not know quite how.

Sophistication may thus encourage paralysis or a crude popularization which defeats its own purpose. The excessively theoretical approach of many research staffs overlooks the problem of the strain of decision-making in times of crisis. What is relevant for policy depends not only on academic truth but also on what can be implemented under stress. The technical staffs are frequently operating in a framework of theoretical standards while in fact their usefulness depends on essentially psychological criteria. To be politically meaningful, their proposals must involve answers to the following types of questions: Does the executive understand the proposal? Does he believe in it? Does he accept it as a guide to action or as an excuse for doing nothing? But if these kinds of concerns are given too much weight, the requirements of salesmanship will defeat substance.

The pragmatism of executives thus clashes with the theoretical bent of research or planning staffs. Executives as a rule take cognizance of a problem only when it emerges as an administrative issue. They thus unwittingly encourage bureaucratic contests as the only means of generating decisions. Or the various elements of the bureaucracy make a series of nonaggression pacts with each other and thus reduce the decision-maker to a benevolent constitutional monarch. As the special role of the executive increasingly becomes to choose between proposals generated administratively, decision-makers turn into arbiters rather than leaders. Whether they wait until a problem emerges as an administrative issue or until a crisis has demonstrated the irrelevance of the standard operating procedure, the modern decision-makers often find themselves the prisoners of their advisers.

Faced with an administrative machine which is both elaborate and fragmented, the executive is forced into essentially lateral means of control. Many of his public pronouncements, though ostensibly directed to outsiders, perform a perhaps more important role in laying down guidelines for the bureaucracy. The chief significance of a foreign policy speech by the President may thus be that it settles an internal debate in Washington (a public statement is more useful for this purpose than an administrative memorandum because it is harder to reverse). At the same time, the bureaucracy's awareness of this method of control tempts it to shortcut its debates by using pronouncements by the decision-makers as charters for special purposes. The executive thus finds himself confronted by proposals for public declarations which may be innocuous in themselves—and whose bureaucratic significance may be anything but obvious—but which can be used by some agency or department to launch a study or program which will restrict his freedom of decision later on.

All of this drives the executive in the direction of extra-bureaucratic means of decision. The practice of relying on special emissaries or personal envoys is an example; their status outside the bureaucracy frees them from some of its restraints. International agreements are sometimes possible only by ignoring safeguards against capricious action. It is a paradoxical aspect of modern bureaucracies that their quest for objectivity and calculability often leads to impasses which can be overcome only by essentially arbitrary decisions.

Such a mode of operation would involve a great risk of stagnation even in "normal" times. It becomes especially dangerous in a revolutionary period. For then, the problems which are most obtrusive may be least relevant. The issues which are most significant may not be suitable for administrative formulation and even when formulated may not lend themselves to bureaucratic consensus. When the issue is how to transform the existing framework, routine can become an additional obstacle to both comprehension and action.

This problem, serious enough *within* each society, is magnified in the conduct of international affairs. While the formal machinery of decision-making in developed countries shows many similarities, the criteria which influence decisions vary enormously. With each administrative machine increasingly absorbed in its own internal problems, diplomacy loses its flexibility. Leaders are extremely aware of the problems of placating their own bureaucracy; they cannot depart too far from its prescriptions without raising serious morale problems. Decisions are reached so painfully that the very anguish of decision-making acts as a brake on the give-and-take of traditional diplomacy.

This is true even *within* alliances. Meaningful consultation with other nations becomes very difficult when the internal process of decision-making already has some of the characteristics of compacts between quasi-sovereign entities. There is an increasing reluctance to hazard a hard-won domestic consensus in an international forum.

What is true within alliances—that is, among nations which have at least some common objectives—becomes even more acute in relations between antagonistic states or blocs. The gap created when two large bureaucracies generate goals largely in isolation from each other and on the basis of not necessarily commensurable criteria is magnified considerably by an ideological schism. The degree of ideological fervor is not decisive; the problem would exist even if the original ideological commitment had declined on either or both sides. The criteria for bureaucratic decision-making may continue to be influenced by ideology even after its élan has dissipated. Bureaucratic structures generate their own momentum which may more than counterbalance the loss of earlier fanaticism. In the early stages of a revolutionary movement, ideology is crucial and the accident of personalities can be decisive. The Reign of Terror in France was ended by the elimination of a single man, Robespierre. The Bolshevik revolution could hardly have taken place had Lenin not been on the famous train which crossed Germany into Russia. But once a revolution becomes institutionalized, the administrative structures which it has spawned develop their own vested interests. Ideology may grow less significant in creating commitment; it becomes pervasive in supplying criteria of administrative choice. Ideologies prevail by being taken for granted. Orthodoxy substitutes for conviction and produces its own form of rigidity.

In such circumstances, a meaningful dialogue across ideological dividing lines becomes extraordinarily difficult. The more elaborate the administrative structure, the less relevant an individual's view becomes—indeed one of the purposes of bureaucracy is to liberate decision-making from the accident of personalities. Thus while personal convictions may be modified, it requires a really monumental effort to alter bureaucratic commitments. And if change occurs, the bureaucracy prefers to move at its own pace and not be excessively influenced by statements or pressures of foreigners. For all these reasons, diplomacy tends to become rigid or to turn into an abstract bargaining process based on largely formal criteria such as "splitting the difference." Either course is self-defeating: the former because it negates the very purpose of diplomacy; the latter because it subordinates purpose to technique and because it may encourage intransigence. Indeed, the incentive for intransigence increases if it is known that the difference will generally be split.

Ideological differences are compounded because major parts of the world are only in the first stages of administrative evolution. Where the technologically advanced countries suffer from the inertia of overadministration, the developing areas often lack even the rudiments of effective bureaucracy. Where the advanced countries may drown in "facts," the emerging nations are frequently without the most elementary knowledge needed for forming a meaningful judgment or for implementing it once it has been taken. Where large bureaucracies operate in alternating spurts of rigidity and catastrophic (in relation to the bureaucracy) upheaval, the new states tend to make decisions on the basis of almost random pressures. The excessive institutionalization of one and the inadequate structure of the other inhibit international stability.

III. THE NATURE OF LEADERSHIP

WHATEVER one's view about the degree to which choices in international affairs are "objectively" determined, the decisions are made by individuals who will be above all conscious of the seeming multiplicity of options. Their understanding of the nature of their choice depends on many factors, including their experience during their rise to eminence.

The mediating, conciliatory style of British policy in the nineteenth century reflected, in part, the qualities encouraged during careers in Parliament and the values of a cohesive leadership group connected by ties of family and common education. The hysterical cast of the policy of Imperial Germany was given impetus by a domestic structure in which political parties were deprived of responsibility while ministers were obliged to balance a monarch by divine right against a Parliament composed of representatives without any prospect of ever holding office. Consensus could be achieved most easily through fits of national passion which in turn disquieted all of Germany's neighbors. Germany's foreign policy grew unstable because its domestic structure did little to discourage capricious improvisations; it may even have put a premium on them.

The collapse of the essentially aristocratic conception of foreign policy of the nineteenth century has made the career experiences of leaders even more crucial. An aristocracy—if it lives up to its values—will reject the arbitrariness of absolutist rule; and it will base itself on a notion of quality which discourages the temptations of demagoguery inherent in plebiscitarian democracy. Where position is felt to be a birthright, generosity is possible (though not guaranteed); flexibility is not inhibited by a commitment to perpetual success. Where a leader's estimate of himself is not completely dependent on his standing in an administrative structure, measures can be judged in terms of a conception of the future rather than of an almost compulsive desire to avoid even a temporary setback. When statesmen belonged to a community transcending national boundaries, there tended to be consensus on the criteria of what constituted a reasonable proposal. This did not prevent conflicts, but it did define their nature and encourage dialogue. The bane of aristocratic foreign policy was the risk of frivolousness, of a self-confidence unrelated to knowledge, and of too much emphasis on intuition.

In any event, ours is the age of the expert or the charismatic leader. The expert has his constituency—those who have a vested interest in commonly held opinions; elaborating and defining its consensus at a high level has, after all, made him an expert. Since the expert is often the product of the administrative dilemmas described earlier, he is usually in a poor position to transcend them. The charismatic leader, on the other hand, needs a perpetual revolution to maintain his position. Neither the expert nor the charismatic leader operates in an environment which puts a premium on long-range conceptions or on generosity or on subordinating the leader's ego to purposes which transcend his own career.

Leadership groups are formed by at least three factors: their experiences during their rise to eminence; the structure in which they must operate; the values of their society. Three contemporary types will be discussed here: (a) the bureau-cratic-pragmatic type, (b) the ideological type, and (c) the revolutionary-charismatic type.

Bureaucratic-pragmatic leadership. The main example of this type of leadership is the American élite—though the leadership groups of other Western countries increasingly approximate the American pattern. Shaped by a society without fundamental social schisms (at least until the race problem became visible) and the product of an environment in which most recognized problems have proved soluble, its approach to policy is *ad hoc,* pragmatic, and somewhat mechanical.

Because pragmatism is based on the conviction that the context of events produces a solution, there is a tendency to await developments. The belief is prevalent that every problem will yield if attacked with sufficient energy. It is inconceivable, therefore, that delay might result in irretrievable disaster; at worst it is thought to require a redoubled effort later on. Problems are segmented into constituent elements, each of which is dealt with by experts in the special difficulty it involves. There is little emphasis or concern for their interrelationship. Technical issues enjoy more careful attention, and receive more sophisticated treatment, than political ones. Though the importance of intangibles is affirmed in theory, it is difficult to obtain a consensus on which factors are significant and even harder to find a meaningful mode for dealing with them. Things are done because one knows how to do them and not because one ought to do them. The criteria for dealing with trends which are conjectural are less well developed than those for immediate crises. Pragmatism, at least in its generally accepted form, is more concerned with method than with judgment; or rather it seeks to reduce judgment to methodology and value to knowledge.

This is reinforced by the special qualities of the professions —law and business—which furnish the core of the leadership groups in America. Lawyers—at least in the Anglo-Saxon tradition—prefer to deal with actual rather than hypothetical cases; they have little confidence in the possibility of stating a future issue abstractly. But planning by its very nature is hypothetical. Its success depends precisely on the ability to transcend the existing framework. Lawyers may be prepared to undertake this task; but they will do well in it only to the extent that they are able to overcome the special qualities encouraged by their profession. What comes naturally to lawyers in the Anglo-Saxon tradition is the sophisticated analysis of a series of *ad hoc* issues which emerge as problems through adversary proceedings. In so far as lawyers draw on the experience which forms them, they have a bias toward awaiting developments and toward operating within the definition of the problem as formulated by its chief spokesmen.

This has several consequences. It compounds the already powerful tendencies within American society to identify foreign policy with the solution of immediate issues. It produces great refinement of issues as they arise, but it also encourages the administrative dilemmas described earlier. Issues are dealt with only as the pressure of events imposes the need for resolving them. Then, each of the contending factions within the bureaucracy has a maximum incentive to state its case in its most extreme form because the ultimate outcome depends, to a considerable extent, on a bargaining process. The premium placed on advocacy turns decision-making into a series of adjustments among special interests—a process more suited to domestic than to foreign policy. This procedure neglects the long range because the future has no administrative constitutency and is, therefore, without representation in the adversary proceedings. Problems tend to be slighted until some agency or department is made responsible for them. When this occurs—usually when a difficulty has already grown acute—the relevant department becomes an all-out spokesman for its particular area of responsibility. The outcome usually depends more on the pressures or the persuasiveness of the contending advocates than on a concept of over-all purpose. While these tendencies exist to some extent in all bureaucracies they are particularly pronounced in the American system of government.

This explains in part the peculiar alternation of rigidity and spasms of flexibility in American diplomacy. On a given issue—be it the Berlin crisis or disarmament or the war in Vietnam—there generally exists a great reluctance to develop a negotiating position or a statement of objectives except in the most general terms. This stems from a desire not to prejudge the process of negotiations and above all to retain flexibility in the face of unforeseeable events. But when an approaching conference or some other pressures make the development of a position imperative and some office or individual is assigned the specific task, a sudden change occurs. Both personal and bureaucratic success are then identified with bringing the particular assignment to a conclusion. Where so much stock is placed in negotiating skill, a failure of a conference may be viewed as a reflection on the ability of the negotiator rather than on the objective difficulty of the subject. Confidence in the bargaining process causes American negotiators to be extremely sensitive to the tactical requirements of the conference table—sometimes at the expense of longer-term considerations. In internal discussions, American negotiators—generally irrespective of their previous commitments—often become advocates for the maximum range of concessions; their legal background tempts them to act as mediators between Washington and the country with which they are negotiating.

The attitudes of the business élite reinforce the convictions of the legal profession. The American business executive rises through a process of selection which rewards the ability to manipulate the known—in itself a conciliatory procedure. The special skill of the executive is thought to consist in coordinating well-defined functions rather than in challenging them. The procedure is relatively effective in the business world, where the executive can often substitute decisiveness, long experience, and a wide range of personal acquaintance for reflectiveness. In international affairs, however—especially in a revolutionary situation—the strong will which is one of our business executives' notable traits may produce essentially arbitrary choices. Or unfamiliarity with the subject matter may have the opposite effect of turning the executive into a spokesman for his technical staffs. In either case, the business executive is even more dependent than the lawyer on the bureaucracy's formulation of the issue. The business élite is even less able or willing than the lawyer to recognize that the formulation of an issue, not the technical remedy, is usually the central problem.

All this gives American policy its particular cast. Problems are dealt with as they arise. Agreement on what constitutes a problem generally depends on an emerging crisis which settles the previously inconclusive disputes about priorities. When a problem is recognized, it is dealt with by a mobilization of all resources to overcome the immediate symptoms. This often

involves the risk of slighting longer-term issues which may
not yet have assumed crisis proportions and of overwhelming,
perhaps even undermining, the structure of the area concerned by a flood of American technical experts proposing
remedies on an American scale. Administrative decisions
emerge from a compromise of conflicting pressures in which
accidents of personality or persuasiveness play a crucial role.
The compromise often reflects the maxim that "if two parties
disagree the truth is usually somewhere in between." But the
pedantic application of such truisms causes the various contenders to exaggerate their positions for bargaining purposes
or to construct fictitious extremes to make their position appear moderate. In either case, internal bargaining predom-
inates over substance.

The *ad hoc* tendency of our decision-makers and the reliance on adversary proceeding cause issues to be stated in
black-and-white terms. This suppresses a feeling for nuance
and makes it difficult to recognize the relationship between
seemingly discrete events. Even with the perspective of a
decade there is little consensus about the relationship between the actions culminating in the Suez fiasco and the
French decision to enter the nuclear field; or about the in-
consistency between the neutralization of Laos and the step-
up of the military effort in Vietnam.

The same quality also produces a relatively low valuation
of historical factors. Nations are treated as similar phenomena, and those states presenting similar immediate problems
are treated similarly. Since many of our policy-makers first
address themselves to an issue when it emerges as their area
of responsibility, their approach to it is often highly anec-
dotal. Great weight is given to what people say and relatively
little to the significance of these affirmations in terms of domestic structure or historical background. Agreement may be

taken at face value and seen as reflecting more consensus than actually exists. Opposition tends to produce moral outrage which often assumes the form of personal animosity—the attitude of some American policy-makers toward President de Gaulle is a good example.

The legal background of our policy-makers produces a bias in favor of constitutional solutions. The issue of supra-nationalism or confederalism in Europe has been discussed largely in terms of the right of countries to make independent decisions. Much less weight has been given to the realities which would limit the application of a majority vote against a major country whatever the legal arrangements. (The fight over the application of Article 19 of the United Nations Charter was based on the same attitude.) Similarly, legal terms such as "integration" and "assignment" sometimes become ends in themselves and thus obscure the operational reality to which they refer. In short, the American leadership groups show high competence in dealing with technical issues, and much less virtuosity in mastering a historical process. And the policies of other Western countries exhibit variations of the American pattern. A lesser pragmatism in continental Europe is counterbalanced by a smaller ability to play a world-role.

The ideological type of leadership. As has been discussed above, the impact of ideology can persist long after its initial fervor has been spent. Whatever the ideological commitment of individual leaders, a lifetime spent in the Communist hierarchy must influence their basic categories of thought— especially since Communist ideology continues to perform important functions. It still furnishes the standard of truth and the guarantee of ultimate success. It provides a means for maintaining cohesion among the various Communist parties of the world. It supplies criteria for the settlement of disputes both within the bureaucracy of individual Communist countries and among the various Communist states.

However attenuated, Communist ideology is, in part, responsible for international tensions. This is less because of specific Marxist tactical prescriptions—with respect to which Communists have shown a high degree of flexibility—than because of the basic Marxist-Leninist categories for interpreting reality. Communist leaders never tire of affirming that Marxism-Leninism is the key element of their self-proclaimed superiority over the outside world; as Marxist-Leninists they are convinced that they understand the historical process better than the non-Communist world does.

The essence of Marxism-Leninism—and the reason that normal diplomacy with Communist states is so difficult—is the view that "objective" factors such as the social structure, the economic process, and, above all, the class struggle are more important than the personal convictions of statesmen. Belief in the predominance of objective factors explains the Soviet approach to the problem of security. If personal convictions are "subjective," Soviet security cannot be allowed to rest on the good will of other statesmen, especially those of a different social system. This produces a quest for what may be described as absolute security—the attempt to be so strong as to be independent of the decisions of other countries. But absolute security for one country means absolute insecurity for all others; it can be achieved only by reducing other states to impotence. Thus an essentially defensive foreign policy can grow indistinguishable from traditional aggression.

The belief in the predominance of objective factors explains why, in the past, periods of détente have proved so precarious. When there is a choice between Western good will or a physical gain, the pressures to choose the latter have been overwhelming. The wartime friendship with the West was sacrificed to the possibility of establishing Communist-controlled governments in Eastern Europe. The spirit of Geneva did not survive the temptations offered by the prospect of undermining the Western position in the Middle East. The many overtures of the Kennedy administration were rebuffed until the Cuban missile crisis demonstrated that the balance of forces was not in fact favorable for a test of strength.

The reliance on objective factors has complicated negotiations between the West and the Communist countries. Communist negotiators find it difficult to admit that they could be swayed by the arguments of men who have, by definition, an inferior grasp of the laws of historical development. No matter what is said, they think that they understand their Western counterpart better than he understands himself. Concessions are possible, but they are made to "reality," not to individuals or to a bargaining process. Diplomacy becomes difficult when one of the parties considers the key element to negotiation—the give-and-take of the process of bargaining—as but a superstructure for factors not part of the negotiation itself.

Finally, whatever the decline in ideological fervor, orthodoxy requires the maintenance of a posture of ideological hostility to the non-Communist world even during a period of coexistence. Thus, in a reply to a Chinese challenge, the Communist Party of the U.S.S.R. declared: "We fully support the destruction of capitalism. We not only believe in the inevitable death of capitalism but we are doing everything possible for it to be accomplished through class struggle as quickly as possible." [2]

The wariness toward the outside world is reinforced by the

2. "The Soviet Reply to the Chinese Letter," open letter of the Central Committee of the Communist Party of the Soviet Union as it appeared in *Pravda*, July 14, 1963, pp. 1–4; *The Current Digest of the Soviet Press* Vol. XV, No. 28 (August 7, 1963), p. 23.

personal experiences which Communist leaders have had on the road to eminence. In a system where there is no legitimate succession, a great deal of energy is absorbed in internal maneuvering. Leaders rise to the top by eliminating—sometimes physically, always bureaucratically—all possible opponents. Stalin had all individuals who helped him into power executed. Khrushchev disgraced Kaganovich, whose protegé he had been, and turned on Marshal Zhukov six months after being saved by him from a conspiracy of his other colleagues. Brezhnev and Kosygin owed their careers to Khrushchev; they nevertheless overthrew him and started a campaign of calumny against him within twenty-four hours of his dismissal.

Anyone succeeding in Communist leadership struggles must be single-minded, unemotional, dedicated, and, above all, motivated by an enormous desire for power. Nothing in the personal experience of Soviet leaders would lead them to accept protestations of good will at face value. Suspiciousness is inherent in their domestic position. It is unlikely that their attitude toward the outside world is more benign than toward their own colleagues or that they would expect more consideration from it.

The combination of personal qualities and ideological structure also affects relations *among* Communist states. Since national rivalries are thought to be the result of class conflict, they are expected to disappear wherever Socialism has triumphed. When disagreements occur they are dealt with by analogy to internal Communist disputes: by attempting to ostracize and then to destroy the opponent. The tendency to treat different opinions as manifestations of heresy causes disagreements to harden into bitter schisms. The debate between Communist China and the U.S.S.R. is in many respects more acrimonious than that between the U.S.S.R. and the non-Communist world.

Even though the basic conceptual categories of Communist leadership groups are similar, the impact of the domestic structure of the individual Communist states on international relations varies greatly. It makes a considerable difference whether an ideology has become institutionalized, as in the Soviet Union, or whether it is still impelled by its early revolutionary fervor, as in Communist China. Where ideology has become institutionalized a special form of pragmatism may develop. It may be just as empirical as that of the United States but it will operate in a different realm of "reality." A different philosophical basis leads to the emergence of another set of categories for the settlement of disputes, and these in turn generate another range of problems.

A Communist bureaucratic structure, however pragmatic, will have different priorities from ours; it will give greater weight to doctrinal considerations and conceptual problems. It is more than ritual when speeches of senior Soviet leaders begin with hour-long recitals of Communist ideology. Even if it were ritual, it must affect the definition of what is considered reasonable in internal arguments. Bureaucratization and pragmatism may lead to a loss of élan; they do not guarantee convergence of Western and Soviet thinking.

The more revolutionary manifestations of Communism, such as Communist China, still possess more ideological fervor, but, paradoxically, their structure may permit a wider latitude for new departures. Tactical intransigence and ideological vitality should not be confused with structural rigidity. Because the leadership bases its rule on a prestige which transcends bureaucratic authority, it has not yet given so many hostages to the administrative structure. If the leadership should change—or if its attitudes are modified—policy could probably be altered much more dramatically in Communist China than in the more institutionalized Communist countries.

The charismatic-revolutionary type of leadership. The contemporary international order is heavily influenced by yet another leadership type: the charismatic revolutionary leader. For many of the leaders of the new nations the bureaucratic-pragmatic approach of the West is irrelevant because they are more interested in the future which they wish to construct than in the manipulation of the environment which dominates the thinking of the pragmatists. And ideology is not satisfactory because doctrine supplies rigid categories which overshadow the personal experiences which have provided the impetus for so many of the leaders of the new nations.

The type of individual who leads a struggle for independence has been sustained in the risks and suffering of such a course primarily by a commitment to a vision which enabled him to override conditions which had seemed overwhelmingly hostile. Revolutionaries are rarely motivated primarily by material considerations—though the illusion that they are persists in the West. Material incentives do not cause a man to risk his existence and to launch himself into the uncertainties of a revolutionary struggle. If Castro or Sukarno had been principally interested in economics, their talents would have guaranteed them a brilliant career in the societies they overthrew. What made their sacrifices worthwhile to them was a vision of the future—or a quest for political power. To revolutionaries the significant reality is the world which they are striving to bring about, not the world they are fighting to overcome.

This difference in perspective accounts for the inconclusiveness of much of the dialogue between the West and many of the leaders of the new countries. The West has a tendency to believe that the tensions in the emerging nations are caused by a low level of economic activity. To the apostles of economic development, raising the gross national product seems the key to political stability. They believe that it should receive the highest priority from the political leaders of new countries and supply their chief motivation.

But to the charismatic heads of many of the new nations, economic progress, while not unwelcome, offers too limited a scope for their ambitions. It can be achieved only by slow, painful, highly technical measures which contrast with the heroic exertions of the struggle for independence. Results are long-delayed; credit for them cannot be clearly established. If Castro were to act on the advice of theorists of economic development, the best he could hope for would be that after some decades he would lead a small progressive country— perhaps a Switzerland of the Caribbean. Compared to the prospect of leading a revolution throughout Latin America, this goal would appear trivial, boring, perhaps even unreal to him.

Moreover, to the extent that economic progress is achieved, it may magnify domestic political instability, at least in its early phases. Economic advance disrupts the traditional political structure. It thus places constant pressures on the incumbent leaders to reestablish the legitimacy of their rule. For this purpose a dramatic foreign policy is particularly apt. Many leaders of the new countries seem convinced that an adventurous foreign policy will not harm prospects for economic development and may even foster it. The competition of the superpowers makes it likely that economic assistance will be forthcoming regardless of the actions of the recipient. Indeed the more obtrusive their foreign policy the greater is their prospect of being wooed by the chief contenders.

The tendency toward a reckless policy is magnified by the

uncertain sense of identity of many of the new nations. National boundaries often correspond to the administrative subdivisions established by the former colonial rulers. States thus have few of the attributes of nineteenth-century European nationalism: common language, common culture, or even common history. In many cases, the only common experience is a century or so of imperial rule. As a result, there is a great pressure toward authoritarian rule, and a high incentive to use foreign policy as a means of bringing about domestic cohesion.

Western-style democracy presupposes that society transcends the political realm; in that case opposition challenges a particular method of achieving common aims but not the existence of the state itself. In many of the new countries, by contrast, the state represents the primary, sometimes the sole, manifestation of social cohesion. Opposition can therefore easily appear as treason—apart from the fact that leaders who have spent several decades running the risks of revolutionary struggle or who have achieved power by a coup d'état are not likely to favor a system of government which makes them dispensable. Indeed the attraction of Communism for many of these leaders is not Marxist-Leninist economic theory but the legitimacy for authoritarian rule which it provides.

No matter what the system of government, many of the leaders of the new nations use foreign policy as a means to escape intractable internal difficulties and as a device to achieve domestic cohesion. The international arena provides an opportunity for the dramatic measures which are impossible at home. These are often cast in an anti-Western mold because this is the easiest way to re-create the struggle against imperial rule which is the principal unifying element for many new nations. The incentive is particularly strong because the rivalry of the nuclear powers eliminates many of the risks which previously were associated with an adventurous foreign policy—especially if that foreign policy is directed against the West, which lacks any effective sanctions.

Traditional military pressure is largely precluded by the nuclear stalemate and respect for world opinion. But the West is neither prepared nor able to use the sanction which weighs most heavily on the new countries: the deliberate exploitation of their weak domestic structure. In many areas the ability to foment domestic unrest is a more potent weapon than traditional arms. Many of the leaders of the new countries will be prepared to ignore the classical panoply of power; but they will be very sensitive to the threat of domestic upheaval. States with a high capacity for exploiting domestic instability can use it as a tool of foreign policy. China, though lacking almost all forms of classical long-range military strength, is a growing factor in Africa. Weak states may be more concerned with a country's capacity to organize domestic unrest in their territory than with its capacity for physical destruction.

Conclusion. Contemporary domestic structures thus present an unprecedented challenge to the emergence of a stable international order. The bureaucratic-pragmatic societies concentrate on the manipulation of an empirical reality which they treat as given; the ideological societies are split between an essentially bureaucratic approach (though in a different realm of reality than the bureaucratic-pragmatic structures) and a group using ideology mainly for revolutionary ends. The new nations, in so far as they are active in international affairs, have a high incentive to seek in foreign policy the perpetuation of charismatic leadership.

These differences are a major obstacle to a consensus on what constitutes a "reasonable" proposal. A common diagnosis of the existing situation is hard to achieve, and it is even more difficult to concert measures for a solution. The situation is complicated by the one feature all types of leadership have in common: the premium put on short-term goals and the domestic need to succeed at all times. In the bureaucratic societies policy emerges from a compromise which often produces the least common denominator, and it is implemented by individuals whose reputation is made by administering the status quo. The leadership of the institutionalized ideological state may be even more the prisoner of essentially corporate bodies. Neither leadership can afford radical changes of course for they result in profound repercussions in its administrative structure. And the charismatic leaders of the new nations are like tightrope artists—one false step and they will plunge from their perch.

IV. DOMESTIC STRUCTURE AND FOREIGN POLICY: THE PROSPECTS FOR WORLD ORDER

MANY contemporary divisions are thus traceable to differences in domestic structure. But are there not countervailing factors? What about the spread of technology and its associated rationality, or the adoption on a global scale of many Western political forms? Unfortunately the process of "Westernization" does not inevitably produce a similar concept of reality. For what matters is not the institutions or the technology, but the significance which is attached to them. And this differs according to the evolution of the society concerned.

The term "nation" does not mean the same thing when applied to such various phenomena as India, France, and Nigeria. Similarly, technology is likely to have a different significance for different peoples, depending on how and when it was acquired.

Any society is part of an evolutionary process which proceeds by means of two seemingly contradictory mechanisms. On the one hand, the span of possible adaptations is delimited by the physical environment, the internal structure, and, above all, by previous choices. On the other hand, evolution proceeds not in a straight line but through a series of complicated variations which appear anything but obvious to the chief actors. In retrospect a choice may seem to have been nearly random or else to have represented the only available alternative. In either case, the choice is not an isolated act but an accumulation of previous decisions reflecting history or tradition and values as well as the immediate pressures of the need for survival. And each decision delimits the range of possible future adaptations.

Young societies are in a position to make radical changes of course which are highly impractical at a later stage. As a society becomes more elaborate and as its tradition is firmly established, its choices with respect to its internal organization grow more restricted. If a highly articulated social unit attempts basic shifts, it runs the risk of doing violence to its internal organization, to its history and values as embodied in its structure. When it accepts institutions or values developed elsewhere it must adapt them to what its structure can absorb. The institutions of any political unit must therefore be viewed in historical context for that alone can give an indication of their future. Societies—even when their institutions are similar—may be like ships passing in the night which find themselves but temporarily in the same place.

Is there then no hope for cooperation and stability? Is our international system doomed to incomprehension and its members to mounting frustration?

It must be admitted that if the domestic structures were considered in isolation, the prognosis would not be too hopeful. But domestic structures do not exist in a vacuum. They must respond to the requirements of the environment. And here all states find themselves face to face with the necessity of avoiding a nuclear holocaust. While this condition does not restrain all nations equally, it nevertheless defines a common task which technology will impose on even more countries as a direct responsibility.

Then, too, a certain similarity in the forms of administration may bring about common criteria of rationality, as Professor Jaguaribe has pointed out.[3] Science and technology will spread. Improved communications may lead to the emergence of a common culture. The fissures between domestic structures and the different stages of evolution are important, but they may be outweighed by the increasing interdependence of humanity.

It would be tempting to end on this note and to base the hope for peace on the self-evidence of the need for it. But this would be too pat. The deepest problem of the contemporary international order may be that most of the debates which form the headlines of the day are peripheral to the basic division described in this essay. The cleavage is not over particular political arrangements—except as symptoms—but between two styles of policy and two philosophical perspectives.

The two styles can be defined as the political as against the revolutionary approach to order or, reduced to personalities, as the distinction between the statesman and the prophet.

The statesman manipulates reality; his first goal is survival; he feels responsible not only for the best but also for the worst conceivable outcome. His view of human nature is wary; he is conscious of many great hopes which have failed, of many good intentions that could not be realized, of selfishness and ambition and violence. He is, therefore, inclined to erect hedges against the possibility that even the most brilliant idea might prove abortive and that the most eloquent formulation might hide ulterior motives. He will try to avoid certain experiments, not because he would object to the results

3. "World Order, Rationality, and Socioeconomic Development," *Daedalus*, Vol. XCV (Spring 1966), pp. 607–626.

if they succeeded, but because he would feel himself responsible for the consequences if they failed. He is suspicious of those who personalize foreign policy, for history teaches him the fragility of structures dependent on individuals. To the statesman, gradualism is the essence of stability; he represents an era of average performance, of gradual change and slow construction.

By contrast, the prophet is less concerned with manipulating than with creating reality. What is possible interests him less than what is "right." He offers his vision as the test and his good faith as a guarantee. He believes in total solutions; he is less absorbed in methodology than in purpose. He believes in the perfectibility of man. His approach is timeless and not dependent on circumstances. He objects to gradualism as an unnecessary concession to circumstance. He will risk everything because his vision is the primary significant reality to him. Paradoxically, his more optimistic view of human nature makes him more intolerant than the statesman. If truth is both knowable and attainable, only immorality or stupidity can keep man from realizing it. The prophet represents an era of exaltation, of great upheavals, of vast accomplishments, but also of enormous disasters.

The encounter between the political and the prophetic approach to policy is always somewhat inconclusive and frustrating. The test of the statesman is the permanence of the international structure under stress. The test of the prophet is inherent in his vision. The statesman will seek to reduce the prophet's intuition to precise measures; he judges ideas on their utility and not on their "truth." To the prophet this approach is almost sacrilegious because it represents the triumph of expediency over universal principles. To the statesman negotiation is the mechanism of stability because it presupposes that maintenance of the existing order is more

important than any dispute within it. To the prophet negotiations can have only symbolic value—as a means of convert-
ing or demoralizing the opponent; truth, by definition,
cannot be compromised.

Both approaches have prevailed at different periods in
history. The political approach dominated European foreign
policy between the end of the religious wars and the French
Revolution and then again between the Congress of Vienna
and the outbreak of World War I. The prophetic mode was
in the ascendant during the great upheavals of the religious
struggles and the period of the French Revolution, and in
the contemporary uprisings in major parts of the world.

Both modes have produced considerable accomplishments,
though the prophetic style is likely to involve the greater
dislocations and more suffering. Each has its nemesis. The
nemesis of the statesman is that equilibrium, though it may
be the condition of stability, does not supply its own motivation; that of the prophet is the impossibility of sustaining a
mood of exaltation without the risk of submerging man in the
vastness of a vision and reducing him to a mere figure to be
manipulated.

As for the difference in philosophical perspective, it may
reflect the divergence of the two lines of thought which since
the Renaissance have distinguished the West from the part of
the world now called underdeveloped (with Russia occupying an intermediary position). The West is deeply committed
to the notion that the real world is external to the observer,
that knowledge consists of recording and classifying data
—the more accurately the better. Cultures which escaped the
early impact of Newtonian thinking have retained the essentially pre-Newtonian view that the real world is almost
completely *internal* to the observer.

Although this attitude was a liability for centuries—because

it prevented the development of the technology and con-
sumer goods which the West enjoyed—it offers great flexibility
with respect to the contemporary revolutionary turmoil. It
enables the societies which do not share our cultural mode to
alter reality by influencing the perspective of the observer—a
process which we are largely unprepared to handle or even to
perceive. And this can be accomplished under contemporary
conditions without sacrificing technological progress. Technology comes as a gift; acquiring it in its advanced form does
not presuppose the philosophical commitment that discovering it imposed on the West. Empirical reality has a much
different significance for many of the new countries than for
the West because in a certain sense they never went through
the process of discovering it (with Russia again occupying an
intermediary position). At the same time, the difference in
philosophical perspective may cause us to seem cold, super-
cilious, lacking in compassion. The instability of the contemporary world order may thus have at its core a philosophical
schism which makes the issues producing most political debates seem largely tangential.

Such differences in style and philosophical perspective are
not unprecedented. What is novel is the global scale on which
they occur and the risks which the failure to overcome them
would entail. Historically, cleavages of lesser magnitude have
been worked out dialectically, with one style of policy or one
philosophical approach dominant in one era only to give way
later to another conception of reality. And the transition was
rarely free of violence. The challenge of our time is whether
we can deal consciously and creatively with what in previous
centuries was adjusted through a series of more or less violent
and frequently catastrophic upheavals. We must construct an
international order *before* a crisis imposes it as a necessity.

This is a question not of blueprints, but of attitudes. In

fact the overconcern with technical blueprints is itself a symp-ton of our difficulties. Before the problem of order can be "dealt" with—even philosophically—we must be certain that the right questions are being asked.

We can point to some hopeful signs. The most sensitive thinkers of the West have recognized that excessive empiri-cism may lead to stagnation. In many of the new countries—and in some Communist ones as well—the second or third generation of leaders is in the process of freeing itself from the fervor and dogmatism of the early revolutionary period and of relating their actions to an environment which they helped to create. But these are as yet only the first tentative signs of progress on a course whose significance is not always understood. Indeed it is characteristic of an age of turmoil that it produces so many immediate issues that little time is left to penetrate their deeper meaning. The most serious problem therefore becomes the need to acquire a sufficiently wide perspective so that the present does not overwhelm the future.

TWO

CENTRAL ISSUES OF
AMERICAN FOREIGN
POLICY

The twentieth century has known little repose. Since the turn of the century, international crises have been increasing in both frequency and severity. The contemporary unrest, although less apocalyptic than the two world wars which spawned it, is even more profoundly revolutionary in nature.

The essence of a revolution is that it appears to contemporaries as a series of more or less unrelated upheavals. The temptation is great to treat each issue as an immediate and isolated problem which once surmounted will permit the fundamental stability of the international order to reassert itself. But the crises which form the headlines of the day are symptoms of deep-seated structural problems. The international system which produced stability for a century collapsed under the impact of two world wars. The age of the superpowers, which temporarily replaced it, is nearing its end. The current international environment is in turmoil because its essential elements are all in flux simultaneously. This essay will concentrate on structural and conceptual problems rather than specific policy issues.

I. THE STRUCTURAL PROBLEM

FOR THE first time, foreign policy has become global. In the past, the various continents conducted their foreign policy essentially in isolation. Throughout much of history, the foreign policy of Europe was scarcely affected by events in Asia. When, in the late eighteenth and nineteenth centuries, the European powers were extending their influence throughout the world, the effective decisions continued to be made in only a few great European capitals. Today, statesmen face the unprecedented problem of formulating policy for well over a hundred countries. Every nation, no matter how insignificant, participates in international affairs. Ideas are transmitted almost instantaneously. What used to be considered domestic events can now have world-wide consequences.

The revolutionary character of our age can be summed up in three general statements: (a) the number of participants in the international order has increased and their nature has altered; (b) their technical ability to affect each other has vastly grown; (c) the scope of their purposes has expanded.

Whenever the participants in the international system change, a period of profound dislocation is inevitable. They can change because new states enter the political system, or because there is a change in values as to what constitutes legitimate rule, or, finally, because of the reduction in influence of some traditional units. In our period, all of these factors have combined. Since the end of the Second World War, several score of new states have come into being. In the nineteenth century the emergence of even a few new nations produced decades of adjustment, and after the First World War, the successor states of the Austro-Hungarian Empire were never assimilated. Our age has yet to find a structure which matches the responsibilities of the new nations to their aspirations.

As the number of participants has increased, technology has multiplied the resources available for the conduct of foreign policy. A scientific revolution has, for all practical purposes, removed technical limits from the exercise of power in foreign policy. It has magnified insecurities because it has made survival seem to depend on the accidents of a technological breakthrough.

This trend has been compounded by the nature of contemporary domestic structures. As long as the states' ability to mobilize resources was limited, the severity of their conflicts had definite bounds. In the eighteenth century, custom restricted the demands rulers by "divine right" could make upon their subjects; a philosophy of minimum government performed the same role through much of the nineteenth century. Our period has seen the culmination of a process started by the French Revolution: the basing of governmental legitimacy on popular support. Even totalitarian regimes are aberrations of a democratic legitimacy; they depend on popular consensus even when they manufacture it through propaganda and pressure. In such a situation, the consensus is decisive; limitations of tradition are essentially irrelevant. It is an ironic result of the democratization of politics that it has enabled states to marshal ever more resources for their competition.

Ideological conflict compounds these instabilities. In the great periods of cabinet diplomacy, diplomats spoke the same language, not only in the sense that French was the lingua franca, but more importantly because they tended to understand intangibles in the same manner. A similar outlook about aims and methods eases the tasks of diplomacy—it may even be a precondition for it. In the absence of such a consensus, diplomats can still meet, but they lose the ability to persuade. More time is spent on defining contending positions than in resolving them. What seems most reasonable to one side will appear most problematical to the other.

When there is ideological conflict, political loyalties no longer coincide with political boundaries. Conflicts among states merge with divisions within nations; the dividing line between domestic and foreign policy begins to disappear. At least some states feel threatened not only by the foreign policy of other countries but also, and perhaps especially, by domestic transformations. A liberalized Communist regime in Prague—which had in no way challenged Soviet preeminence in foreign policy—caused the Kremlin to believe that its vital interests were threatened and to respond by occupying the country without even the pretext of legality.

The tensions produced by ideological conflict are exacerbated by the reduction in influence of the states that were considered great powers before the First World War. The world has become militarily bipolar. Only two powers—the United States and the Union of Soviet Socialist Republics— possess the full panoply of military might. Over the next decade, no other country or group of countries will be capable of challenging their physical preeminence. Indeed, the gap in military strength between the two giant nuclear countries and the rest of the world is likely to increase rather than diminish over that period.

Military bipolarity is a source of rigidity in foreign policy. The guardians of the equilibrium of the nineteenth century were prepared to respond to change with counteradjustment; the policy-makers of the superpowers in the second half of the twentieth century have much less confidence in the ability of the equilibrium to right itself after disturbance. Whatever "balance" there is between the superpowers is regarded as both precarious and inflexible. A bipolar world loses the perspective for nuance; a gain for one side appears as an absolute loss for the other. Every issue seems to involve a question of survival. The smaller countries are torn between a desire for protection and a wish to escape big-power dominance. Each of the superpowers is beset by the desire to maintain its preeminence among its allies, to increase its influence among the uncommitted, and to enhance its security vis-à-vis its opponent. The fact that some of these objectives may well prove incompatible adds to the strain on the international system.

But the age of the superpowers is now drawing to an end. Military bipolarity has not only failed to prevent, it has actually encouraged political multipolarity. Weaker allies have good reason to believe that their defense is in the overwhelming interest of their senior partner. Hence, they see no need to purchase its support by acquiescence in its policies. The new nations feel protected by the rivalry of the superpowers, and their nationalism leads to ever bolder assertions of self-will. Traditional uses of power have become less feasible, and new forms of pressure have emerged as a result of transnational loyalties and weak domestic structures.

This political multipolarity does not necessarily guarantee

stability. Rigidity is diminished, but so is manageability. Nationalism may succeed in curbing the preeminence of the superpowers; it remains to be seen whether it can supply an integrating concept more successfully in this century than in the last. Few countries have the interest and only the superpowers have the resources to become informed about global issues. As a result, diplomacy is often geared to domestic politics and more concerned with striking a pose than contributing to international order. Equilibrium is difficult to achieve among states widely divergent in values, goals, expectations, and previous experience.

The greatest need of the contemporary international system is an agreed concept of order. In its absence, the awesome available power is unrestrained by any consensus as to legitimacy; ideology and nationalism, in their different ways, deepen international schisms. Many of the elements of stability which characterized the international system in the nineteenth century cannot be re-created in the modern age. The stable technology, the multiplicity of major powers, the limited domestic claims, and the frontiers which permitted adjustments are gone forever. A new concept of international order is essential; without it stability will prove elusive.

This problem is particularly serious for the United States. Whatever our intentions or policies, the fact that the United States disposes of the greatest single aggregate of material power in the world is inescapable. A new international order is inconceivable without a significant American contribution. But the nature of this contribution has altered. For the two decades after 1945, our international activities were based on the assumption that technology plus managerial skills gave us the ability to reshape the international system and to bring about domestic transformations in "emerging countries." This direct "operational" concept of international order has proved too simple. Political multipolarity makes it impossible to impose an American design. Our deepest challenge will be to evoke the creativity of a pluralistic world, to base order on political multipolarity even though overwhelming military strength will remain with the two superpowers.

II. THE LIMITS OF BIPOLARITY: THE NATURE OF POWER IN THE MODERN PERIOD

THROUGHOUT history, military power was considered the final recourse. Statesmen treated the acquisition of additional power as an obvious and paramount objective. As recently as twenty-five years ago, it would have been inconceivable that a country could possess *too much* strength for effective political use; every increment of power was—at least theoretically—politically effective. The minimum aim was to assure the impermeability of the territory. Until the Second World War, a state's strength could be measured by its ability to protect its population from attack.

The nuclear age has destroyed this traditional measure. Increasing strength no longer necessarily confers the ability to protect the population. No foreseeable force level—not even full-scale ballistic missile defenses—can prevent levels of damage eclipsing those of the two world wars. In these conditions, the major problem is to discipline power so that it bears a rational relationship to the objectives likely to be in dispute. The paradox of contemporary military strength is that a gargantuan increase in power has eroded its relationship to policy. The major nuclear powers are capable of devastating

59

each other. But they have great difficulty translating this capability into policy except to prevent direct challenges to their own survival—and this condition is interpreted with increasing strictness. The capacity to destroy is difficult to translate into a plausible threat even against countries with no capacity for retaliation. The margin of superiority of the superpowers over the other states is widening; yet other nations have an unprecedented scope for autonomous action. In relations with many domestically weak countries, a radio transmitter can be a more effective form of pressure than a squadron of B-52s. In other words, power no longer translates automatically into influence. This does not mean that impotence increases influence, only that power does not automatically confer it.

This state of affairs has profound consequences for traditional notions of balance of power. In the past, stability has always presupposed the existence of an equilibrium of power which prevented one state from imposing its will on the others.

The traditional criteria for the balance of power were territorial. A state could gain overwhelming superiority only by conquest; hence, as long as territorial expansion was foreclosed, or severely limited, the equilibrium was likely to be preserved. In the contemporary period, this is no longer true. Some conquests add little to effective military strength; major increases in power are possible entirely through developments within the territory of a sovereign state. China gained more in real military power through the acquisition of nuclear weapons than if it had conquered all of Southeast Asia. If the Soviet Union had occupied Western Europe but had remained without nuclear weapons, it would be less powerful than it is now with its existing nuclear arsenal within its present borders. In other words, the really fundamental changes in the balance of power have all occurred *within* the territorial limits of sovereign states. Clearly, there is an urgent need to analyze just what is understood by power—as well as by balance of power—in the nuclear age.

This would be difficult enough were technology stable. It becomes enormously complicated when a scientific revolution produces an upheaval in weapons technology at five-year intervals. Slogans like "superiority," "parity," "assured destruction," compete unencumbered by clear definitions of their operational military significance, much less a consensus on their political implications. The gap between experts and decision-makers is widening.

In short, as power has grown more awesome, it has also turned abstract, intangible, elusive. Deterrence has become the dominant military policy. But deterrence depends above all on psychological criteria. It seeks to keep an opponent from a given course by posing unacceptable risks. For purposes of deterrence, the opponent's calculations are decisive. A bluff taken seriously is more useful than a serious threat interpreted as a bluff. For political purposes, the meaningful measurement of military strength is the assessment of it by the other side. Psychological criteria vie in importance with strategic doctrine.

The abstract nature of modern power affects domestic disputes profoundly. Deterrence is tested negatively by things which do *not* happen. But it is never possible to demonstrate *why* something has not occurred. Is it because we are pursuing the best possible policy or only a marginally effective one? Bitter debate even among those who believe in the necessity of defense policy is inevitable and bound to be inconclusive. Moreover, the longer peace is maintained—or the more successful deterrence is—the more it furnishes arguments for those who are opposed to the very premises of defense policy. Perhaps there was no need for preparedness in the first place because the opponent never meant to attack. In the modern state, national security is likely to be a highly divisive domestic issue.

The enormity of modern power has destroyed its cumulative impact to a considerable extent. Throughout history the use of force set a precedent; it demonstrated a capacity to use power for national ends. In the twentieth century any use of force sets up inhibitions against resorting to it again. Whatever the outcome of the war in Vietnam, it is clear that it has greatly diminished American willingness to become involved in this form of warfare elsewhere. Its utility as a precedent has therefore been importantly undermined.

The difficulty of forming a conception of power is paralleled by the problem of how to use it diplomatically. In the past, measures to increase readiness signaled the mounting seriousness with which an issue was viewed.[1] But such measures have become less obvious and more dangerous when weapons are always at a high state of readiness—solid-fuel missiles require less than ten minutes to be fired—and are hidden either under the ground or under the oceans. With respect to nuclear weapons, signaling increased readiness has to take place in a narrow range between the danger of failure and the risk of a preemptive strike.

Even when only conventional weapons are involved, the question of what constitutes a politically meaningful threat is increasingly complicated. After the capture of the *Pueblo,* the United States called up thirteen thousand reservists and moved an aircraft carrier into the waters off the shores of Korea. Did the fact that we had to call up reserves when challenged by a fifth-rate military power convey that we

---

1. Sometimes these measures got out of control; the mobilization schedules were one of the principal reasons for the outbreak of the First World War.

meant to act or that we were overextended? Did the move of the aircraft carrier indicate a decision to retaliate or was it intended primarily to strike a pose?

The problem is illustrated dramatically by the war in Vietnam. A massive breakdown of communication occurred not only within the policy-making machinery in the United States but also between the United States and Hanoi. Over the past five years, the U.S. government has found it difficult, if not impossible, to define what it understood by victory. President Johnson extended an open-ended offer for unconditional negotiations. Yet our troops were deployed as if this offer had not been made. The deployment was based on purely military considerations; it did not take into account the possibility that our troops might have to support a negotiation—the timing of which we had, in effect, left to the opponent. Strategy divorced from foreign policy proved sterile.

These perplexities have spurred new interest in arms-control negotiations, especially those dealing with strategic missiles. These negotiations can be important for the peace and security of the world. But to be effective, they require an intellectual resolution of the issues which have bedeviled the formulation of military policy. Unless we are able to give an operational meaning to terms such as "superiority" or "stability," negotiations will lack criteria by which to judge progress.

Thus, whatever the course—a continuation of the arms race or arms control—a new look at American national security policy is essential. Over ten years have passed since the last comprehensive, bipartisan, high-level reevaluation of all aspects of national security: the Gaither Committee. A new administration should move quickly to bring about such a review. It should deal with some of the following problems:
(a) a definition of the national interest and national security

over the next decade; (b) the nature of military power in that period; (c) the relationship of military power to political influence; (d) implications and feasibility (both military and political) of various postures—superiority, parity, and so on; (e) the implications (both political and military) of new developments such as MIRV (multiple individually targeted reentry vehicles) and ballistic missile defenses; (f) the prospects for arms control, including specific measures to moderate the arms race.

III. POLITICAL MULTIPOLARITY: THE CHANGED NATURE OF ALLIANCES

No AREA of policy illustrates more dramatically the tensions between political multipolarity and military bipolarity than the field of alliance policy. For a decade and a half after the Second World War, the United States identified security with alliances. A global network of relationships grew up based on the proposition that deterrence of aggression required the largest possible grouping of powers.

This system of alliances was always in difficulty outside the Atlantic area because it tried to apply principles drawn from the multipolar world of the eighteenth and nineteenth centuries when several major powers of roughly equal strength existed. Then, indeed, it was impossible for one country to achieve dominance if several others combined to prevent it. But this was not the case in the era of the superpowers of the forties and fifties. Outside Europe, our allies added to our strength only marginally; they were in no position to reinforce each other's capabilities.

Alliances, to be effective, must meet four conditions: (1) a common objective—usually defense against a common danger; (2) a degree of joint policy at least sufficient to define the *casus belli;* (3) some technical means of cooperation in case common action is decided upon; (4) a penalty for noncooperation—that is, the possibility of being refused assistance must exist—otherwise protection will be taken for granted and the mutuality of obligation will break down.

In the system of alliances developed by the United States after the Second World War, these conditions have never been met outside the North Atlantic Treaty Organization (NATO). In the Southeast Asia Treaty Organization (SEATO) and the Central Treaty Organization (CENTO), to which we belong in all but name, there has been no consensus as to the danger. Pakistan's motive for obtaining U.S. arms was not security against a Communist attack but protection against India. The Arab members of CENTO armed not against the U.S.S.R. but against Israel. Lacking a conception of common interests, the members of these alliances have never been able to develop common policies with respect to issues of war and peace. Had they been able to do so, such policies might well have been stillborn anyway, because the technical means of cooperation have been lacking. Most allies have neither the resources nor the will to render mutual support. A state which finds it difficult to maintain order or coherence of policy at home does not increase its strength by combining with states suffering similar disabilities.

In these circumstances, SEATO and CENTO have grown moribund as instruments of collective action. Because the United States has often seemed more eager to engage in the defense of its SEATO and CENTO allies than they themselves, they have become convinced that noncooperation will have no cost. In fact, they have been able to give the impression that it would be worse for us than for them if they fell to Communism. SEATO and CENTO have become, in effect, unilateral American guarantees. At best, they provide a legal basis for bilateral U.S. aid.

The case is different with NATO. Here we are united with countries of similar traditions and domestic structures. At the start, there was a common conception of the threat. The technical means for cooperation existed. Mechanisms for developing common policies came into being—especially in the military field. Thus in its first decade and a half, NATO was a dynamic and creative institution.

Today, however, NATO is in disarray as well. Actions by the United States—above all, frequent unilateral changes of policy—are partially responsible. But the most important cause is the transformation of the international environment, specifically the decline in the preeminence of the superpowers and the emergence of political multipolarity. Where the alliances outside of Europe have never been vital because they failed to take into account the military bipolarity of the fifties, NATO is in difficulties because it has yet to adjust to the political multipolarity of the late sixties.

When NATO was founded in 1949, Europeans had a dual fear: the danger of an imminent Soviet attack and the prospect of eventual U.S. withdrawal. In the late 1960s, however, the fear of Soviet invasion has declined. Even the attack on Czechoslovakia is likely to restore anxiety about Soviet military aggression only temporarily. At the same time, two decades of American military presence in Europe coupled with American predominance in NATO planning have sharply reduced the fear that America might wash its hands of European concerns.

When NATO was formed, moreover, the principal threat to world peace seemed to lie in a Soviet attack on Europe. In recent years, the view has grown that equally grave risks are likely to arise in trouble spots outside Europe. To most Europeans, these do not appear as immediate threats to their independence or security. The irony here is striking. In the fifties, Europeans were asking for American assistance in Asia and the Middle East with the argument that they were defending the greater interests of freedom. The United States replied that these very interests required American aloofness. Today, the roles are precisely reversed. It is Europe that evades our entreaties to play a global role; that is to say, Europeans do not consider their interests at stake in America's extra-European involvement.

These are symptoms of deeper, structural problems, however. One problem, paradoxically, is the growth of European economic strength and political self-confidence. At the end of the Second World War, Europe was dependent on the United States for economic assistance, political stability, and military protection. As long as Europe needed the shelter of a super-power, American predominance was inevitable. In relations with the United States, European statesmen acted as lobbyists rather than as diplomats. Their influence depended less on the weight of their countries than on the impact of their personalities. A form of consultation evolved whereby Europeans sought to influence American actions by giving us a reputation to uphold or—to put it more crudely—by oscillating between flattery and almost plaintive appeals for reassurance. The United States, secure in its predominance, in turn concentrated on soothing occasional European outbreaks of insecurity rather than on analyzing their causes.

Tutelage is a comfortable relationship for the senior partner, but it is demoralizing in the long run. It breeds illusions of omniscience on one side and attitudes of impotent irresponsibility on the other. In any event, the United States could not expect to perpetuate the accident of Europe's postwar exhaustion into a permanent pattern of international relations. Europe's economic recovery inevitably led to a return to more traditional political pressures.

These changes in Europe were bound to lead to a difficult transitional period. They could have resulted in a new partnership between the United States and an economically resurgent and politically united Europe, as had been envisaged by many of the early advocates of Atlantic unity. However, the European situation has not resolved itself in that way. Thoughtful Europeans know that Europe must unite in some form if it is to play a major role in the long run. They are aware, too, that Europe does not make even approximately the defense effort of which it is capable. But European unity is stymied, and domestic politics has almost everywhere dominated security policy. The result is a massive frustration which expresses itself in special testiness toward the United States.

These strains have been complicated by the growth of Soviet nuclear power. The changed nature of power in the modern period has affected NATO profoundly. As the risks of nuclear war have become enormous, the credibility of traditional pledges of support has inevitably been reduced. In the past, a country would carry out a commitment because, it could plausibly be argued, the consequences of not doing so were worse than those of coming to the ally's assistance. This is no longer self-evident. In each of the last three annual statements by the Secretary of Defense on the U.S. defense posture, the estimate of *dead* in a general nuclear war ranged from 40 to 120 million. This figure will, if anything, increase. It will become more and more difficult to demonstrate that *anything* is worse than the elimination of over half of a society in a matter of days. The more NATO relies on strategic nuclear war as a counter to all forms of attack, the less credible its pledges will be.

The consciousness of nuclear threat by the two superpowers

has undermined allied relationships in yet another way. For understandable reasons, the superpowers have sought to make the nuclear environment more predictable—witness the nuclear test ban treaty and the nonproliferation treaty. But the blind spot in our policy has been the failure to understand that, in the absence of full consultation, our allies see in these talks the possible forerunner of a more comprehensive arrangement affecting their vital interests negotiated without them. Strategic arms talks thus emphasize the need of political understanding in acute form. The pattern of negotiating an agreement first and then giving our allies an opportunity— even a full one—to comment is intolerable in the long run. It puts the onus of failure on them, and it prevents them from doing more than quibble about a framework with which they may disagree. Strains have been reinforced by the uncertain American response to the Soviet invasion of Czechoslovakia— especially the reluctance to give up the prospect of a summit meeting. Atlantic relations, for all their seemingly normalcy, thus face a profound crisis.

This state of affairs has been especially difficult for those Americans who deserve most credit for forging existing Atlantic relations. Two decades of hegemony have produced the illusion that present Atlantic arrangements are "natural," that wise policy consists of making the existing framework more tolerable. "Leadership" and "partnership" are invoked, but the content given to these words is usually that which will support the existing pattern. European unity is advocated to enable Europeans to share burdens on a world-wide scale.

Such a view fails to take into account the realities of political multipolarity. The aim of returning to the "great days of the Marshall Plan" is impossible. Nothing would sunder Atlantic relationships so surely as the attempt to reassert the notions of leadership appropriate to the early days of NATO.

In the bipolar world of the forties and fifties, order could be equated with military security; integrated command arrangements sufficed as the principal bond of unity. In the sixties, security, while still important, has not been enough. Every crisis from Berlin to Czechoslovakia has seen the call for "strengthening NATO" confined to military dispositions. Within months a malaise has become obvious again because the overriding need for a common political conception has not been recognized. The challenge of the seventies will be to forge unity with political measures.

It is not "natural" that the major decisions about the defense of an area so potentially powerful as Western Europe should be made three thousand miles away. It is not "normal" that Atlantic policies should be geared to American conceptions. In the forties and fifties, practicing unity—through formal resolutions and periodic reassurances—was profoundly important as a symbol of the end of our isolationism. In the decade ahead, we cannot aim at unity as an end in itself; it must emerge from common conceptions and new structures.

"Burden-sharing" will not supply that impetus. Countries do not assume burdens because it is fair, only because it is necessary. While there are strong arguments for Atlantic partnership and European unity, enabling Europe to play a global role is not one of them. A nation assumes responsibilities not only because it has resources but because it has a certain view of its own destiny. Through the greater part of its history—until the Second World War—the United States possessed the resources but not the philosophy for a global role. Today, the poorest Western European country—Portugal —has the widest commitments outside Europe because its historic image of itself has become bound up with its overseas possessions. This condition is unlikely to be met by any other European country—with the possible exception of Great

Britain—no matter what its increase in power. Partially as the result of decolonization, Europeans are unlikely to conduct a significant global policy whatever their resources or their degree of unity. Cooperation between the United States and Europe must concentrate on issues within the Atlantic area rather than global partnership.

Even within the Atlantic area, a more equitable distribution of responsibilities has two prerequisites: there must be some consensus in the analysis of the international situation, at least as it affects Europe; there must be a conviction that the United States cannot or will not carry all the burdens alone. Neither condition is met today. The traditional notion of American leadership tends to stifle European incentives for autonomy. Improved consultation—the remedy usually proposed—can only alleviate, not remove, the difficulty.

The problem of consultation is complex, of course. No doubt unilateral American action has compounded the uneasiness produced by American predominance and European weakness. The shift in emphasis of American policy, from the NATO multilateral force to the nonproliferation treaty, and frequent unilateral changes in strategic doctrine, have all tended to produce disquiet and to undermine the domestic position of ministers who had staked their futures on supporting the American viewpoint.

It is far from self-evident, however, that more extensive consultation within the existing framework can be more than a palliative. One problem concerns technical competence. In any large bureaucracy—and an international consultative process has many similarities to domestic administrative procedures—the weight given to advice bears some relation to the competence it reflects. If one partner possesses all the technical competence, the process of consultation is likely to remain barren. The minimum requirement for effective consultation is that each ally have enough knowledge to give meaningful advice.

But there are even more important limits to the process of consultation. The losing party in a domestic dispute has three choices: (a) it can accept the setback with the expectation of winning another battle later on—this is the usual bureaucratic attitude and it is based on the assurance of another hearing; (b) if advice is consistently ignored, it can resign and go into opposition; (c) as the opposition party, it can have the purpose either of inducing the existing government to change its course or of replacing it. If all these avenues are closed, violence or mounting frustration are the consequences.

Only the first option is open to sovereign states bound together by an alliance, since they obviously cannot resign or go into opposition without wrecking the alliance. They cannot affect the process by which their partners' decision-makers are chosen despite the fact that this may be crucial for their fate. Indeed, as long as the need to maintain the alliance overrides all other concerns, disagreement is likely to be stifled. Advice without responsibility and disagreement without an outlet can turn consultation into a frustrating exercise which compounds rather than alleviates discord.

Consultation is especially difficult when it lacks an integrating over-all framework. The consultation about the non-proliferation treaty concerned specific provisions but not the underlying general philosophy which was of the deepest concern to many of our allies, especially Italy and the Federal Republic of Germany. During periods of détente, each ally makes its own approach to Eastern Europe or the U.S.S.R. without attempting to further a coherent Western enterprise. During periods of crisis, there is pressure for American reassurance but not for a clearly defined common philosophy. In these circumstances, consultation runs the risk of being irrelevant. The issues it "solves" are peripheral; the central issues are inadequately articulated. It deals haphazardly in answers to undefined questions.

Such a relationship is not healthy in the long run. Even with the best will, the present structure encourages American unilateralism and European irresponsibility. This is a serious problem for the United States. If the United States remains the trustee of every non-Communist area, it will exhaust its psychological resources. No country can act wisely simultaneously in every part of the globe at every moment of time. A more pluralistic world—especially in relationships with friends—is profoundly in our long-term interest. Political multipolarity, while difficult to get used to, is the precondition for a new period of creativity. Painful as it may be to admit, we could benefit from a counterweight that would discipline our occasional impetuosity and, by supplying historical perspective, modify our penchant for abstract and "final" solutions.

All of this suggests that there is no alternative to European unity either for the United States or for Europe. In its absence, the malaise can only be alleviated, not ended. Ultimately, this is a problem primarily for the Europeans. In the recent past, the United States has often defeated its purposes by committing itself to one particular form of European unity —that of federalism. It has also complicated British membership in the Common Market by making it a direct objective of American policy.

In the next decade the architectonic approach to Atlantic policy will no longer be possible. The American contribution must be more philosophical; it will have to consist more of understanding and quiet, behind-the-scenes encouragement than of the propagation of formal institutional structures. Involved here is the American conception of how nations cooperate. A tradition of legalism and habits of predominance have produced a tendency to multiply formal arrangements.

But growing European autonomy forces us to learn that nations cooperate less because they have a legal obligation to do so than because they have common purposes. Command arrangements cannot substitute for common interests. Coordinated strategy will be empty unless it reflects shared political concepts. The chance of disagreements on peripheral issues may be the price for unity on issues that really matter. The memory of European impotence and American tutelage should not delude us into believing that we understand Europe's problems better than it does itself. Third-force dangers are not avoided by legal formulas, and, more important, they have been overdrawn. It is hard to visualize a "deal" between the Soviet Union and Europe which would jeopardize our interests without jeopardizing European interests first. In any event, a sense of responsibility in Europe will be a much better counter to Soviet efforts to undermine unity than American tutelage.

In short, our relations with Europeans are better founded on developing a community of interests than on the elaboration of formal legal obligations. No precise blueprint for such an arrangement is possible because different fields of activity have different needs. In the military sphere, for example, modern technology will impose a greater degree of integration than is necessary in other areas. Whatever their formal autonomy, it is almost inconceivable that our allies would prefer to go to war without the support of the United States, given the relatively small nuclear forces in prospect for them. Close coordination between Europe and the United States in the military sphere is dictated by self-interest, and Europe has more to gain from it than the United States.

For this very reason, it is in our interest that Europeans

should assume much greater responsibility for developing doctrine and force levels in NATO, perhaps by vitalizing such institutions as the West European Union (WEU), perhaps by alternative arrangements. The Supreme Allied Commander should in time be a European.

Military arrangements are not enough, however. Under current conditions, no statesman will risk a cataclysm simply to fulfill a legal obligation. He will do so only if a degree of *political* cooperation has been established which links the fate of each partner with the survival of all the others. This requires an entirely new order of political creativity.

Coordination is especially necessary in East-West relations. The conventional view is that NATO can be as useful an instrument for détente as for defense. This is doubtful—at least in NATO's present form. A military alliance, one of the chief cohesive links of which is its integrated command arrangement, is not the best instrument for flexible diplomacy. Turning NATO into an instrument of détente might reduce its security contribution without achieving a relaxation of tensions. A diplomatic confrontation of NATO and the Warsaw Pact would have all the rigidities of the bipolar military world. It would raise fears in Western Europe of an American-Soviet condominium, and it would tend to legitimize the Soviet hegemonical position in Eastern Europe. Above all, it would fail to take advantage of the flexibility afforded by greater Western European unity and autonomy. As Europe gains structure, its attraction for Eastern Europe is bound to increase. The major initiatives to improve relations between Western and Eastern Europe should originate in Europe with the United States in a reserve position.

Such an approach can work only if there is a real consensus as to objectives. Philosophical agreement can make possible flexibility of method. This will require a form of consultation much more substantial than that which now exists and a far more effective and coherent European contribution.

To be sure, events in Czechoslovakia demonstrate the limits of Eastern European autonomy that the Soviet Union is now prepared to tolerate. But the Soviet Union may not be willing indefinitely to use the Red Army primarily against allies as it has done three times in a decade and a half. In any event, no Western policy can guarantee a more favorable evolution in Central Europe; all it can do is to take advantage of an opportunity if it arises.

Policy outside Europe is likely to be divergent. Given the changed European perspective, an effort to bring about global burden-sharing might only produce stagnation. The allies would be able to agree primarily on doing nothing. Any crisis occurring anywhere would turn automatically and organically world-wide. American acceptance of European autonomy implies also European acceptance of a degree of American autonomy with respect to areas in which, for understandable reasons, European concern has lessened.

There may be opportunities for cooperation in hitherto purely national efforts—for example, our space program. European participation in it could help to remedy the "technological gap."

Finally, under present circumstances, an especially meaningful community of interests can be developed in the social sphere. All modern states face problems of bureaucratization, pollution, environmental control, urban growth. These problems know no national considerations. If the nations of the Atlantic work together on these issues—through either private or governmental channels or both—a new generation habituated to cooperative efforts could develop similar to that spawned in different circumstances by the Marshall Plan.

It is high time that the nations bordering the Atlantic deal

—formally, systematically, and at the highest level—with questions such as these: (a) What are the relative roles of Europe and the United States in East-West contacts? (b) Is a division of functions conceivable in which Western Europe plays the principal role in relation to Eastern Europe while the United States concentrates on relationships with the U.S.S.R.? (c) What forms of political consultation does this require? (d) In what areas of the world is common action possible? Where are divergent courses indicated? How are differences to be handled?

Thus, we face the root questions of a multipolar world. How much unity should we want? How much diversity can we stand? These questions never have a final answer within a pluralistic society. Adjusting the balance between integration and autonomy will be the key challenge of emerging Atlantic relations.

IV. BIPOLARITY AND MULTIPOLARITY: THE CONCEPTUAL PROBLEM

IN THE YEARS ahead, the most profound challenge to American policy will be philosophical: to develop some concept of order in a world which is bipolar militarily but multipolar politically. But a philosophical deepening will not come easily to those brought up in the American tradition of foreign policy.

Our political society was one of the few which was *consciously* created at a point in time. At least until the emergence of the race problem, we were blessed by the absence of conflicts between classes and over ultimate ends. These factors produced the characteristic aspects of American foreign policy: a certain manipulativeness and pragmatism, a conviction that the normal pattern of international relations was harmonious, a reluctance to think in structural terms, a belief in final answers—all qualities which reflect a sense of self-sufficiency not far removed from a sense of omnipotence. Yet the contemporary dilemma is that there are no total solutions; we live in a world gripped by revolutions in technology, values, and institutions. We are immersed in an unending process, not in a quest for a final destination. The deepest

79

problems of equilibrium are not physical but psychological or moral. The shape of the future will depend ultimately on convictions which far transcend the physical balance of power.

The New Nations and Political Legitimacy. This challenge is especially crucial with respect to the new nations. Future historians are likely to class the confusion and torment in the emerging countries with the great movements of religious awakening. Continents which had been dormant for centuries suddenly develop political consciousness. Regions which for scores of years had considered foreign rule as natural struggle for independence. Yet it is a curious nationalism which defines itself not as in Europe by common language or culture but often primarily by the common experience of foreign rule. Boundaries—especially in Africa—have tended to follow the administrative convenience of the colonial powers rather than linguistic or tribal lines. The new nations have faced problems both of identity and of political authority. They often lack social cohesiveness entirely, or they are split into competing groups, each with a highly developed sense of identity.

It is no accident that between the Berlin crisis and the invasion of Czechoslovakia, the principal threats to peace came from the emerging areas. Domestic weakness encourages foreign intervention. The temptation to deflect domestic dissatisfactions into foreign adventures is ever present. Leaders feel little sense of responsibility to an over-all international equilibrium; they are much more conscious of their local grievances. The rivalry of the superpowers offers many opportunities for blackmail.

Yet their relations with other countries are not the most significant aspect of the turmoil of the new countries. It is in the new countries that questions of the purpose of political life and the meaning of political legitimacy—key issues also in the modern state—pose themselves in their most acute form. The new nations weigh little in the physical balance of power. But the forces unleashed in the emergence of so many new states may well affect the moral balance of the world—the convictions which form the structure for the world of tomorrow. This adds a new dimension to the problem of multipolarity.

Almost all of the new countries suffer from a revolutionary malaise: revolutions succeed through the coming together of all resentments. But the elimination of existing structures compounds the difficulty of establishing political consensus. A successful revolution leaves as its legacy a profound dislocation. In the new countries, contrary to all revolutionary expectations, the task of construction emerges as less glamorous and more complex than the struggle for freedom; the exaltation of the quest for independence cannot be perpetuated. Sooner or later, positive goals must replace resentment of the former colonial power as a motive force. In the absence of autonomous social forces, this unifying role tends to be performed by the state.

But the assumption of this role by the state does not produce stability. When social cohesiveness is slight, the struggle for control of authority is correspondingly more bitter. When government is the principal, sometimes the sole, expression of national identity, opposition comes to be considered treason. The profound social or religious schisms of many of the new nations turn the control of political authority quite literally into a matter of life and death. Where political obligation follows racial, religious, or tribal lines, self-restraint breaks down. Domestic conflicts assume the character of civil war. Such traditional authority as exists is personal or feudal. The problem is to make it "legitimate"—to develop a notion of political obligation which depends on legal norms rather than on coercive power or personal loyalty.

This process took centuries in Europe. It must be accomplished in decades in the new nations, where preconditions of success are less favorable than at comparable periods in Europe. The new countries are subject to outside pressures; there is a premium on foreign adventures to bring about domestic cohesiveness. Their lack of domestic structure compounds the already great international instabilities.

The American role in the new nations' efforts to build legitimate authority is in need of serious reexamination. The dominant American view about political structure has been that it will follow more or less automatically upon economic progress and that it will take the form of constitutional democracy.

Both assumptions are subject to serious questions. In every advanced country, political stability preceded rather than emerged from the process of industrialization. Where the rudiments of popular institutions did not exist at the beginning of the Industrial Revolution, they did not receive their impetus from it. To be sure, representative institutions were broadened and elaborated as the countries prospered, but their significant features antedated economic development and are not attributable to it. In fact, the system of government which brought about industrialization—whether popular or authoritarian—has tended to be confirmed rather than radically changed by this achievement.

Nor is democracy a natural evolution of nationalism. In the last century, democracy was accepted by a ruling class whose estimate of itself was founded outside the political process. It was buttressed by a middle class, holding a political philosophy in which the state was considered to be a referee of the ultimately important social forces rather than the principal focus of national consciousness. Professional revolutionaries were rarely involved; their bias is seldom democratic.

The pluralism of the West had many causes which cannot be duplicated elsewhere. These included a church organization outside the control of the state and therefore symbolizing the limitation of government power; the Greco-Roman philosophical tradition of justice based on human dignity, reinforced later by the Christian ethic; an emerging bourgeoisie; a stalemate in religious wars imposing tolerance as a practical necessity and a multiplicity of states. Industrialization was by no means the most significant of these factors. Had any of the others been missing, the Western political evolution could have been quite different.

This is why Communism has never succeeded in the industrialized Western countries for which its theory was devised; its greatest successes have been in developing societies. This is no accident. Industrialization—in its early phases—multiplies dislocations. It smashes the traditional framework. It requires a system of values which makes the sacrifices involved in capital formation tolerable and which furnishes some integrating principles to contain psychological frustrations.

Communism is able to supply legitimacy for the sacrifices inseparably connected with capital formation in an age when the maxims of laissez faire are no longer acceptable. And Leninism has the attraction of providing a rationale for holding on to power. Many of the leaders of the new countries are revolutionaries who sustained themselves through the struggle for independence by visions of the transformations to be brought about after victory. They are not predisposed even to admit the possibility of giving up power in their hour of triumph. Since they usually began their struggle for independence while in a small minority and sustained it against heavy odds, they are not likely to be repelled by the notion that it is possible to "force men to be free."

The ironic feature of the current situation is that Marxism, professing a materialistic philosophy, is accepted only where it does not exist: in some new countries and among protest movements of the advanced democratic countries. Its appeal is its idealistic component and not its economic theory. It offers a doctrine of substantive change and an explanation of final purposes. Its philosophy has totally failed to inspire the younger generation in Communist countries, where its bureaucratic reality is obvious.

On the other hand, the United States, professing an idealistic philosophy, often fails to gain acceptance for democratic values because of its heavy reliance on economic factors. It has answers to technical dislocations but has not been able to contribute much to building a political and moral consensus. It offers a procedure for change but little content for it.

The problem of political legitimacy is the key to political stability in regions containing two-thirds of the world's population. A stable domestic system in the new countries will not automatically produce international order, but international order is impossible without it. An American agenda must include some conception of what we understand by political legitimacy. In an age of instantaneous communication, we cannot pretend that what happens to over two-thirds of humanity is of no concern or interest to the United States. This does not mean that our goal should be to transfer American institutions to the new nations—even less that we should impose them. Nor should we define the problem as how to prevent the spread of Communism. Our goal should be to build a moral consensus which can make a pluralistic world creative rather than destructive.

Irrelevance to one of the great revolutions of our time will mean that we will ultimately be engulfed by it—if not physically, then psychologically. Already some of the protest movements have made heroes of leaders in repressive new countries. The absurdity of founding a claim for freedom on protagonists of the totalitarian state—such as Guevara or Ho or Mao—underlines the impact of the travail of the new countries on older societies which share none of their technical but some of their spiritual problems, especially the problem of the nature of authority in the modern world. To a young generation in rebellion against bureaucracy and bored with material comfort, these societies offer at least the challenge of unlimited opportunity (and occasionally unlimited manipulativeness) in the quest for justice.

A world which is bipolar militarily and multipolar politically thus confronts an additional problem. Side by side with the physical balance of power, there exists a psychological balance based on intangibles of value and belief. The presuppositions of the physical equilibrium have changed drastically; those of the psychological balance remain to be discovered.

The Problem of Soviet Intentions. Nothing has been more difficult for Americans to assimilate in the nuclear age than the fact that even enmity is complex. In the Soviet Union, we confront an opponent whose public pronouncements are insistently hostile. Yet the nuclear age imposes a degree of cooperation and an absolute limit to conflicts.

The military relationship with the Soviet Union is difficult enough; the political one confronts us with a profound conceptual problem. A society which regards peace as the normal condition tends to ascribe tension not to structural causes but to wicked or shortsighted individuals. Peace is thought to result either from the automatic operation of economic forces or from the emergence of a more benign leadership abroad.

The debate about Soviet trends between "hard-liners" and "soft-liners" illustrates this problem. Both sides tend to agree that the purpose of American policy is to encourage a more benign evolution of Soviet society—the original purpose of containment was, after all, to bring about the *domestic* transformation of the U.S.S.R. They are at one that a settlement presupposes a change in the Soviet system. Both groups imply that the nature of a possible settlement is perfectly obvious. But the apostles of containment have never specified the American negotiating program to be undertaken from the position of strength their policy was designed to achieve. The advocates of relaxation of tensions have been no more precise; they have been more concerned with atmosphere than with the substance of talks.

In fact, the difference between the "hawks" and "doves" has usually concerned timing: the hawks have maintained that a Soviet change of heart, while inevitable, was still in the future, whereas the doves have argued that it has already taken place. Many of the hawks tend to consider all negotiations as fruitless. Many of the doves argue—or did before Czechoslovakia—that the biggest step toward peace has already been accomplished by a Soviet change of heart about the cold war; negotiations need only remove some essentially technical obstacles.

The difference affects—and sometimes poisons—the entire American debate about foreign policy. Left-wing critics of American foreign policy seem incapable of attacking U.S. actions without elevating our opponent (whether it happens to be Mao or Castro or Ho) to a pedestal. If they discern some stupidity or self-interest on our side, they assume that the other side must be virtuous. They then criticize the United States for opposing the other side. The right follows the same logic in reverse: they presuppose *our* good intentions and conclude that the other side must be perverse in opposing us.

Both the left and the right judge largely in terms of intentions. In the process, whatever the issue—whether Berlin or Vietnam—more attention is paid to whether to get to the conference room than what to do once we arrive there. The dispute over Communist intentions has diverted attention from elaborating our own purposes. In some quarters, the test of dedication to peace has been whether one interprets Soviet intentions in the most favorable manner.

It should be obvious, however, that the Soviet domestic situation is complex and its relationship to foreign policy far from obvious. It is true that the risks of general nuclear war should be as unacceptable to Moscow as to Washington; but this truism does not automatically produce détente. It also seems to lessen the risks involved in local intervention. No doubt the current generation of Communist leaders lacks the ideological dynamism of their predecessors who made the revolution; at the same time, they have at their disposal a military machine of unprecedented strength, and they must deal with a bureaucracy of formidable vested interests. Unquestionably, Soviet consumers press their leaders to satisfy their demands; but it is equally true that an expanding modern economy is able to supply *both* guns and butter. Some Soviet leaders may have become more pragmatic; but in an elaborated Communist state, the results of pragmatism are complex. Once power is seized and industrialization is largely accomplished, the Communist Party faces a difficult situation. It is not needed to conduct the government, and it has no real function in running the economy (though it tries to do both). In order to justify its continued existence and command, it may develop a vested interest in vigilance against outside danger and thus in perpetuating a fairly high level of tension.

It is beyond the scope of this essay to go into detail on the issue of internal Communist evolution. But it may be appropriate to inquire why, in the past, every period of détente has proved stillborn. There have been at least five periods of peaceful coexistence since the Bolshevik seizure of power, one in each decade of the Soviet state. Each was hailed in the West as ushering in a new era of reconciliation and as signifying the long-awaited final change in Soviet purposes. Each ended abruptly with a new period of intransigence, which was generally ascribed to a victory of Soviet hard-liners rather than to the dynamics of the system. There were undoubtedly many reasons for this. But the tendency of many in the West to be content with changes of Soviet tone and to confuse atmosphere with substance surely did not help matters. It has enabled the Communist leaders to postpone the choice which they must make sooner or later: whether to use détente as a device to lull the West or whether to move toward a resolution of the outstanding differences. As long as this choice is postponed, the possibility exists that latent crises may run away with the principal protagonists, as happened in the Middle East and perhaps even in Czechoslovakia.

The eagerness of many in the West to emphasize the liberalizing implications of Soviet economic trends and to make favorable interpretation of Soviet intentions a test of good faith may have the paradoxical consequence of strengthening the Soviet hard-liners. Soviet troops had hardly arrived in Prague when some Western leaders began to insist that the invasion would not affect the quest for détente while others continued to indicate a nostalgia for high-level meetings. Such an attitude hardly serves the cause of peace. The risk is great that if there is no penalty for intransigence there is no incentive for conciliation. The Kremlin may use negotiations —including arms control—as a safety valve to dissipate Western suspicions rather than as a serious endeavor to resolve concrete disputes or to remove the scourge of nuclear war.

If we focus our policy discussions on Soviet purposes, we confuse the debate in two ways: Soviet trends are too ambiguous to offer a reliable guide—it is possible that not even Soviet leaders fully understand the dynamics of their system; it deflects us from articulating the purposes we should pursue, whatever Soviet intentions. Peace will not, in any event, result from one grand settlement but from a long diplomatic process, and this process requires some clarity as to our destination. Confusing foreign policy with psychotherapy deprives us of criteria by which to judge the political foundations of international order.

The obsession with Soviet intentions causes the West to be smug during periods of détente and panicky during crises. A benign Soviet tone is equated with the achievement of peace; Soviet hostility is considered to be the signal for a new period of tension and usually evokes purely military countermeasures. The West is thus never ready for a Soviet change of course; it has been equally unprepared for détente and intransigence.

These lines are being written while outrage at the Soviet invasion of Czechoslovakia is still strong. There is a tendency to focus on military implications or to speak of strengthening unity in the abstract. But if history is a guide, there will be a new Soviet peace offensive sooner or later. Thus, reflecting about the nature of détente seems most important while its achievement appears most problematical. If we are not to be doomed to repeat the past, it may be well to learn some of its lessons: we should not again confuse a change of tone with a change of heart. We should not pose false inconsistencies between allied unity and détente; indeed, a true relaxation of tensions presupposes Western unity. We should concentrate negotiations on the concrete issues that threaten peace, such as intervention in the third world. Moderating the arms race must also be high on the agenda. None of this is possible without a concrete idea of what we understand by peace and a creative world order.

V. AN INQUIRY INTO THE
AMERICAN NATIONAL INTEREST

WHEREVER we turn, then, the central task of American foreign policy is to analyze anew the current international environment and to develop some concepts which will enable us to contribute to the emergence of a stable order.

First, we must recognize the existence of profound structural problems that are to a considerable extent independent of the intentions of the principal protagonists and that cannot be solved merely by good will. The vacuum in Central Europe and the decline of the Western European countries would have disturbed the world equilibrium regardless of the domestic structure of the Soviet Union. A strong China has historically tended to establish suzerainty over its neighbors; in fact, one special problem of dealing with China—Communism apart—is that it has had no experience in conducting foreign policy with equals. China has been either dominant or subjected.

To understand the structural issue, it is necessary to undertake an inquiry, from which we have historically shied away, into the essence of our national interest and into the premises of our foreign policy. It is part of American folklore that, while other nations have interests, we have responsibilities; while other nations are concerned with equilibrium, we are concerned with the legal requirements of peace. We have a tendency to offer our altruism as a guarantee of our reliability: "We have no quarrel with the Communists," Secretary of State Rusk said on one occasion; "all our quarrels are on behalf of other people."

Such an attitude makes it difficult to develop a conception of our role in the world. It inhibits other nations from gearing their policy to ours in a confident way—a "disinterested" policy is likely to be considered "unreliable." A mature conception of our interest in the world would obviously have to take into account the widespread interest in stability and peaceful change. It would deal with two fundamental questions: What is it in our interest to prevent? What should we seek to accomplish?

The answer to the first question is complicated by an often-repeated proposition that we must resist aggression anywhere it occurs since peace is indivisible. A corollary is the argument that we do not oppose the fact of particular changes but the method by which they are brought about. We find it hard to articulate a truly vital interest which we would defend however "legal" the challenge. This leads to an undifferentiated globalism and confusion about our purposes. The abstract concept of aggression causes us to multiply our commitments. But the denial that our interests are involved diminishes our staying power when we try to carry out these commitments.

Part of the reason for our difficulties is our reluctance to think in terms of power and equilibrium. In 1949, for example, a State Department memorandum justified NATO as follows: "[The treaty] obligates the parties to defend the purposes and principles of the United Nations, the freedom, common heritage and civilization of the parties and their free

institutions based upon the principles of democracy, individual liberty and the role of law. It obligates them to act in
defense of peace and security. It is directed against no one; it
is directed solely against aggression. It seeks not to influence
any shifting balance of power but to strengthen a balance of
principle."

But principle, however lofty, must at some point be related
to practice; historically, stability has always coincided with an
equilibrium that made physical domination difficult. Interest
is not necessarily amoral; moral consequences can spring from
interested acts. Britain did not contribute any the less to international order for having a clear-cut concept of its interest
which required it to prevent the domination of the Continent
by a single power (no matter in what way it was threatened)
and the control of the seas by anybody (even if the immediate
intentions were not hostile). A new American administration
confronts the challenge of relating our commitments to our
interests and our obligations to our purposes.

The task of defining positive goals is more difficult but even
more important. The first two decades after the end of the
Second World War posed problems well suited to the American approach to international relations. Wherever we turned,
massive dislocations required attention. Our pragmatic, *ad
hoc* tendency was an advantage in a world clamoring for
technical remedies. Our legal bent contributed to the development of many instruments of stability.

In the late sixties, the situation is more complex. The
United States is no longer in a position to operate programs
globally; it has to encourage them. It can no longer impose its
preferred solution; it must seek to evoke it. In the forties and
fifties, we offered remedies; in the late sixties and in the
seventies our role will have to be to contribute to a structure
that will foster the initiative of others. We are a superpower

physically, but our designs can be meaningful only if they generate willing cooperation. We can continue to contribute to defense and positive programs, but we must seek to encourage and not stifle a sense of local responsibility. Our contribution should not be the sole or principal effort, but it should make the difference between success and failure.

This task requires a different kind of creativity and another form of patience than we have displayed in the past. Enthusiasm, belief in progress, and the invincible conviction that American remedies can work everywhere must give way to an understanding of historical trends, an ordering of our preferences, and above all an understanding of the difference our preferences can in fact make.

The dilemma is that there can be no stability without equilibrium but, equally, equilibrium is not a purpose with which we can respond to the travail of our world. A sense of mission is clearly a legacy of American history; to most Americans, America has always stood for something other than its own grandeur. But a clearer understanding of America's interests and of the requirements of equilibrium can give perspective to our idealism and lead to humane and moderate objectives, especially in relation to political and social change. Thus our conception of world order must have deeper purposes than stability but greater restraints on our behavior than would result if it were approached only in a fit of enthusiasm.

Whether such a leap of the imagination is possible in the modern bureaucratic state remains to be seen. New administrations come to power convinced of the need for goals and for comprehensive concepts. Sooner, rather than later, they find themselves subjected to the pressures of the immediate and the particular. Part of the reason is the pragmatic, issue-oriented bias of our decision-makers. But the fundamental reason may be the pervasiveness of modern bureaucracy.

What started out as an aid to decision-making has developed a momentum of its own. Increasingly, the policy-maker is more conscious of the pressures and the morale of his staff than of the purpose this staff is supposed to serve. The policy-maker becomes a referee among quasi-autonomous bureaucratic bodies. Success consists of moving the administrative machinery to the point of decision, leaving relatively little energy for analyzing the decision's merit. The modern bureaucratic state widens the range of technical choices while limiting the capacity to make them.

An even more serious problem is posed by the change of ethic of precisely the most idealistic element of American youth. The idealism of the fifties during the Kennedy era expressed itself in self-confident, often zealous, institution building. Today, however, many in the younger generation consider the management of power irrelevant, perhaps even immoral. While the idea of service retains a potent influence, it does so largely with respect to problems which are clearly *not* connected with the strategic aspects of American foreign policy; the Peace Corps is a good example. The new ethic of freedom is not "civic"; it is indifferent or even hostile to systems and notions of order. Management is equated with manipulation. Structural designs are perceived as systems of "domination"—not of order. The generation which has come of age after the fifties has had Vietnam as its introduction to world politics. It has no memory of occasions when American-supported structural innovations were successful or of the motivations which prompted these enterprises.

Partly as a result of the generation gap, the American mood oscillates dangerously between being ashamed of power and expecting too much of it. The former attitude deprecates the use or possession of force; the latter is overly receptive to the possibilities of absolute action and overly indifferent to the likely consequences. The danger of a rejection of power is that it may result in a nihilistic perfectionism which disdains the gradual and seeks to destroy what does not conform to its notion of utopia. The danger of an overconcern with force is that policy-makers may respond to clamor by a series of spasmodic gestures and stylistic maneuvers and then recoil before their implications.

These essentially psychological problems cannot be overemphasized. It is the essence of a satisfied, advanced society that it puts a premium on operating within familiar procedures and concepts. It draws its motivation from the present, and it defines excellence by the ability to manipulate an established framework. But for the major part of humanity, the present becomes endurable only through a vision of the future. To most Americans—including most American leaders —the significant reality is what they see around them. But for most of the world—including many of the leaders of the new nations—the significant reality is what they wish to bring about. If we remain nothing but the managers of our physical patrimony, we will grow increasingly irrelevant. And since there can be no stability without us, the prospects of world order will decline.

We require a new burst of creativity, however, not so much for the sake of other countries as for our own people, especially the youth. The contemporary unrest is no doubt exploited by some whose purposes are all too clear. But that it is there to exploit is proof of a profound dissatisfaction with the merely managerial and consumer-oriented qualities of the modern state and with a world which seems to generate crises by inertia. The modern bureaucratic state, for all its panoply of strength, often finds itself shaken to its foundations by seemingly trivial causes. Its brittleness and the world-wide revolution of youth—especially in advanced countries and among the relatively affluent—suggest a spiritual void, an almost metaphysical boredom with a political environment that increasingly emphasizes bureaucratic challenges and is dedicated to no deeper purpose than material comfort.

Our unrest has no easy remedy. Nor is the solution to be found primarily in the realm of foreign policy. Yet a deeper nontechnical challenge would surely help us regain a sense of direction. The best and most prideful expressions of American purposes in the world have been those in which we acted in concert with others. Our influence in these situations has depended on achieving a reputation as a member of such a concert. To act consistently abroad we must be able to generate coalitions of shared purposes. Regional groupings supported by the United States will have to take over major responsibility for their immediate areas, with the United States being concerned more with the over-all framework of order than with the management of every regional enterprise.

In the best of circumstances, the next administration will be beset by crises. In almost every area of the world, we have been living off capital—warding off the immediate, rarely dealing with underlying problems. These difficulties are likely to multiply when it becomes apparent that one of the legacies of the war in Vietnam will be a strong American reluctance to risk overseas involvements.

A new administration has the right to ask for compassion and understanding from the American people. But it must found its claim not on pat technical answers to difficult issues; it must above all ask the right questions. It must recognize that, in the field of foreign policy, we will never be able to contribute to building a stable and creative world order unless we first form some conception of it.

THREE

THE VIETNAM
NEGOTIATIONS

The Paris peace negotiations have been marked by the classic Vietnamese syndrome: optimism alternating with bewilderment; euphoria giving way to frustration. The halt to the bombing produced another wave of high hope. Yet a civil war which has torn a society for twenty years and which has involved the great powers is unlikely to be settled in a single, dramatic stroke. Even if there were mutual trust—a commodity not in excessive supply—the complexity of the issues and the difficulty of grasping their interrelationship would make for complicated negotiations. Throughout the war, criteria by which to measure progress have been hard to come by; this problem has continued during the negotiations. The dilemma is that almost any statement about Vietnam is likely to be true; unfortunately, truth does not guarantee relevance.

I. THE SITUATION
WITHIN SOUTH VIETNAM
PRIOR TO NEGOTIATIONS

THE SEQUENCE of events that led to negotiations probably started with General Westmoreland's visit to Washington in November 1967. On that occasion, General Westmoreland told a Joint Session of Congress that the war was being militarily won. He outlined "indicators" of progress and stated that a limited withdrawal of United States combat forces might be undertaken beginning late in 1968. On January 17, 1968, President Johnson, in his State of the Union address, emphasized that the pacification program—the extension of the control of Saigon into the countryside—was progressing satisfactorily. Sixty-seven percent of the population of Vietnam lived in relatively secure areas; the figure was expected to rise. A week later, the Tet offensive overthrew the assumptions of American strategy.

What had gone wrong? The basic problem has been conceptual: the tendency to apply traditional maxims of both strategy and "nation building" to a situation which they did not fit.

American military strategy followed the classic doctrine that victory depended on a combination of control of territory and attrition of the opponent. Therefore, the majority of the American forces were deployed along the frontiers of South Vietnam to prevent enemy infiltration and in the Central Highlands where most of the North Vietnamese main force units—those units organized along traditional military lines—were concentrated. The theory was that defeat of the main forces would cause the guerrillas to wither on the vine. Victory would depend on inflicting casualties substantially greater than what we suffered until Hanoi's losses became "unacceptable."

This strategy suffered from two disabilities: (a) the nature of guerrilla warfare, (b) the asymmetry in the definition of what constituted unacceptable losses. A guerrilla war differs from traditional military operation because its key prize is not control of territory but control of the population. This depends, in part, on psychological criteria, especially a sense of security. No positive program can succeed unless the population feels safe from terror or reprisal. Guerrillas rarely seek to hold real estate; their tactic is to use terror and intimidation to discourage cooperation with constituted authority.

The distribution of the population in Vietnam makes this problem particularly acute. Over ninety percent of the population lives in the coastal plain and the Mekong Delta; the Central Highlands and the frontiers, on the other hand, are essentially unpopulated. Eighty percent of American forces came to be concentrated in areas containing less than four percent of the population; the locale of military operations was geographically removed from that of the guerrilla conflict. As North Vietnamese theoretical writings never tired of pointing out, the United States could not hold territory and protect the population simultaneously. By opting for military victory through attrition, the United States strategy produced what came to be the characteristic feature of the Vietnamese war: military successes that could not be translated into permanent political advantage. (Even the goal of stopping infiltration was very hard to implement in the trackless, nearly impenetrable jungles along the Cambodian and Laotian frontiers.)

As a result, the American conception of security came to have little in common with the experience of the Vietnamese villagers. American maps classified areas by three categories of control, neatly shown in various colors: government, contested, and Viet Cong. The formal criteria were complicated, and depended to an unusual extent on reports by officers whose short term of duty (barely twelve months) made it next to impossible for them to grasp the intangibles and nuances which constitute the real elements of control in the Vietnamese countryside. In essence, the first category included all villages which contained some governmental authority; "contested" referred to areas slated to be entered by governmental cadres. The American notion of security was a reflection of Western administrative theory; control was assumed to be in the hands of one of the contestants more or less exclusively.

But the actual situation in Vietnam was quite different; a realistic security map would have shown few areas of exclusive jurisdiction; the pervasive experience of the Vietnamese villager was the ubiquitousness of both sides. Saigon controlled much of the country in the daytime, in the sense that government troops could move anywhere if they went in sufficient force; the Viet Cong dominated a large part of the same population at night. For the villagers, the presence of government during the day had to be weighed against its absence after dark when Saigon's cadres almost invariably withdrew into the district or provincial capitals. If armed teams of administrators considered the villages unsafe at night, the villagers could hardly be expected to resist the guerrillas. Thus, the typical pattern in Vietnam has been dual control, with the villagers complying with whatever force was dominant during a particular part of the day.

The political impact of this dual control was far from symmetrical, however. To be effective, the government had to demonstrate a very great capacity to provide protection, probably well over ninety percent. The guerrillas' aim was largely negative: to prevent the consolidation of governmental authority. They did not need to destroy all governmental programs—indeed in some areas they made no effort to interfere with them. They did have to demonstrate a capability to punish individuals who threw in their lot with Saigon. An occasional assassination or raid served to shake confidence for months afterwards.

The North Vietnamese and Viet Cong had another advantage which they used skillfully. American "victories" were empty unless they laid the basis for an eventual withdrawal. The North Vietnamese and Viet Cong, fighting in their own country, needed merely to keep in being forces sufficiently strong to dominate the population after the United States tired of the war. We fought a military war; our opponents fought a political one. We sought physical attrition; our opponents aimed for our psychological exhaustion. In the process, we lost sight of one of the cardinal maxims of guerrilla war: the guerrilla wins if he does not lose; the conventional army loses if it does not win. The North Vietnamese used their main forces the way a bullfighter uses his cape—to keep us lunging into areas of marginal political importance.

The United States strategy of attrition failed to reduce the guerrillas and was in difficulty even with respect to the North Vietnamese main forces. Since Hanoi made no attempt to hold any territory, and since the terrain of the Central Highlands cloaked North Vietnamese movements, it proved difficult to make the opposing forces fight except at places which they chose. Indeed, a considerable majority of engagements came to be initiated by the other side; this enabled Hanoi to regulate its casualties (and ours) at least within certain limits. The so-called "kill-ratios" of United States to North Vietnamese casualties became highly unreliable indicators. They were falsified further because the level of what was "unacceptable" to Americans fighting thousands of miles from home turned out to be much lower than that of Hanoi fighting on Vietnamese soil.

All this caused our military operations to have little relationship to our declared political objectives. Progress in establishing a political base was excruciatingly slow; our diplomacy and our strategy were conducted in isolation from each other. President Johnson had announced repeatedly that we would be ready to negotiate, unconditionally, at any moment, anywhere. This, in effect, left the timing of negotiations to the other side. But short of a complete collapse of the opponent, our military deployment was not well designed to support a negotiation. For purposes of negotiations, we would have been better off with one hundred percent control over sixty percent of the country (to give us a bargaining counter), than with sixty percent control of one hundred percent of the country.

The effort to strengthen Saigon's political control faced other problems. To be meaningful, the so-called pacification program had to meet two conditions: (a) it had to provide security for the population, (b) it had to establish a political and institutional link between the villages and Saigon. Neither condition was ever met: impatience to show "progress" in the strategy of attrition caused us to give low priority to protection of the population; in any event, there was no concept as to how to bring about a political framework relating Saigon to the countryside. As a result, economic programs had to carry an excessive load. Economic programs had produced stability in Europe because existing political and administrative structures were threatened above all by the gap between expectations and reality. In Vietnam—as in most developing countries—the overwhelming problem is not to *buttress* but to *develop* a political framework. Economic progress by undermining the existing patterns of obligation—which are generally personal or feudal—serves to accentuate the need for political institutions. One ironic aspect of the war in Vietnam is that while we profess an idealistic philosophy, our failures have been due to an excessive reliance on material factors. The Communists, by contrast, holding to a materialistic interpretation, owe many of their successes to their ability to supply an answer to the question of the nature and foundation of political authority.

The Tet offensive brought the compounded weaknesses—or, as the North Vietnamese say, the internal contradictions—of the American position to a head. To be sure, from a strictly military point of view, the offensive was an American victory. Viet Cong casualties were very large; in many provinces, the Viet Cong infrastructure of guerrillas and shadow administrators surfaced and could be severely mauled by American forces. But in a guerrilla war, purely military considerations are not decisive: psychological and political factors loom at least as large.

On that level the Tet offensive was a political defeat in the countryside for Saigon and the United States. Two claims had been pressed on the villages. The United States and Saigon had promised that they would be able to protect an ever larger number of villages. The Viet Cong had never claimed that they were able to provide permanent protection; they had claimed that they were the real power and presence in the villages and they threatened those who collaborated with Saigon or the United States with retribution.

As happened so often in the past, the Viet Cong made their claim stick. Some twenty provincial capitals were occupied. Though the Viet Cong held none (except Hue) for more than a few days, they were there long enough to execute hundreds of Vietnamese on the basis of previously prepared lists. While the words "secure area" never had the same significance for Vietnamese civilians as for Americans, it applied most meaningfully to the provincial and district capitals. This was precisely where the Tet offensive took its most severe toll. The Viet Cong had made a point whose importance far transcends military considerations: there are no secure areas for Vietnamese civilians. This has compounded the already great tendency of the Vietnamese population to await developments and not to commit itself irrevocably to the Saigon government. The withdrawal of government troops from the countryside to protect cities and the consequent increase in Viet Cong activity in the villages even in the daytime has served to strengthen this trend.

For all these reasons, the Tet offensive marked the watershed of the American effort. Henceforth, no matter how effective our actions, the prevalent strategy could no longer achieve its objectives in a period or with force levels politically acceptable to the American people. This realization caused Washington, for the first time, to put a ceiling on the number of troops for Vietnam. Denied the very large additional forces requested, the military command in Vietnam felt obliged to begin a gradual change of its peripheral strategy to one concentrating on the protection of the populated areas. This made inevitable an eventual commitment to a political solution and marked the beginning of the quest for a negotiated settlement. Thus, the stage was set for President Johnson's speech of March 31, which ushered in the current negotiations.

II. THE ENVIRONMENT
OF NEGOTIATIONS

OF COURSE, the popular picture that negotiations began in May is only partially correct. The United States and Hanoi have rarely been out of touch since the American commitment in Vietnam started to escalate. Not all these contacts have been face to face. Some have been by means of public pronouncements. Between 1965 and 1968, the various parties publicly stated their positions in a variety of forums: Hanoi announced Four Points, the NLF put forth Five Points, Saigon advanced Seven Points, and the United States—perhaps due to its larger bureaucracy—promulgated Fourteen.

These public pronouncements produced a fairly wide area of apparent agreement on some general principles—that the Geneva accords could form the basis of a settlement, that American forces would be withdrawn ultimately, that the reunification of Vietnam should come about through direct negotiation between the Vietnamese, that (after a settlement) Vietnam not contain foreign bases. The United States has indicated that three of Hanoi's Four Points are acceptable.[1]

1. These are: withdrawal of United States forces, the provision of the Geneva agreements calling for neutrality for North and South Vietnam,

There is disagreement about the status of Hanoi's forces in the South; indeed Hanoi has yet to admit that it has forces in the South—though it has prepared a "fall-back position" to the effect that North Vietnamese forces in the South cannot be considered "external." The role of the NLF is equally in dispute. Saigon rejects a separate political role for the NLF; the NLF considers Saigon a puppet regime. There is no agreement about the meaning of those propositions which sound alike or on how they are to be enforced.

In addition to negotiations by public pronouncements, there have been secret contacts which have been described in many books and articles.[2] It has been alleged that these contacts have failed because of a lack of imagination or a failure of coordination within our government. (There have also been charges of deliberate sabotage.) A fair assessment of these criticisms will not be possible for many years. But it is clear that many critics vastly oversimplify the problem. Good will may not always have been present; but even were it to motivate all sides, rapid, dramatic results would be unlikely, for all parties face enormous difficulties. Indeed, the tendency of each side to overestimate the freedom to maneuver of the other has almost certainly compounded distrust. It has caused Hanoi to appear perversely obstinate to Washington and Washington to seem ostentatiously devious to Hanoi.

Both Hanoi and the United States are limited in their freedom of action by the state of mind of the population of South Vietnam, which will ultimately determine the outcome

---

and reunification on the basis of popular wishes. The United States has rejected the third point, which implies that the internal arrangements for South Vietnam should be settled on the basis of the NLF program—though the United States has agreed to consider the NLF program among others.

2. The fullest account is to be found in Kraslow and Loory, *The Secret Search for Peace in Vietnam* (New York: Random House, 1968).

of the conflict. The Vietnamese people have lived under foreign rule for approximately half of their history. They have maintained a remarkable cultural and social cohesion by being finely attuned to the realities of power. To survive, the Vietnamese have had to learn to calculate—almost instinctively—the real balance of forces. If negotiations give the impression of being a camouflaged surrender, there will be nothing left to negotiate. Support for the side which seems to be losing will collapse. Thus, all the parties are aware—Hanoi explicitly, for it does not view war and negotiations as separate processes; we in a more complicated bureaucratic manner—that *the way* negotiations are carried out is almost as important as *what* is negotiated. The choreography of how one enters negotiations, what is settled first, and in what manner is inseparable from the substance of the issues.

Wariness is thus imposed on the negotiators; a series of deadlocks is difficult to avoid. There are no "easy" issues for each issue is symbolic and therefore in a way prejudges the final settlement. On its merits, the debate about the site of the conference—extending over a period of four weeks in April and May—was trivial. Judged intellectually, the four weeks were "wasted." But they did serve a useful function: they enabled the United States to let Saigon get used to the idea that there *would* be negotiations and to maintain that it retained control over events. It would not be surprising if Hanoi had a similar problem with the NLF.

The same problem was illustrated by the way the decision to stop the bombing was presented. Within twenty-four hours, both Hanoi and Saigon made statements of extraordinary bellicosity which, taken literally, would have doomed the substantive talks about to begin. But their real purpose was to reassure each side's supporters in the South. Saigon especially has had a difficult problem. It has been pictured by many as perversely stubborn because of its haggling over the status of the NLF. However, to Saigon, the status of the NLF cannot be a procedural matter. For South Vietnam it has been very nearly the central issue of the war. Washington must bear at least part of the responsibility for underestimating the depth and seriousness of this concern.

The situation confronted by Washington and Hanoi internationally is scarcely less complex. Much of the bitter debate in the United States about the war in Vietnam has been conducted in terms of the categories of 1961 and 1962. Unquestionably, the failure to analyze adequately the geopolitical importance of Vietnam then contributed to the current dilemma. But the commitment of five hundred thousand Americans has settled the issue of the importance of Vietnam. For what is involved now is confidence in American promises. However fashionable it is to ridicule the terms "credibility" or "prestige," they are not empty phrases; other nations can gear their actions to ours only if they can count on our steadiness.

No doubt the Vietnamese war is highly unpopular in many countries—though the intensity of the criticism seems to increase with distance from the scene. It does not follow that we can remove the charge of bad judgment by a demonstration of incompetence. Even critics are unlikely to be reassured by a complete collapse of the American effort in Vietnam. Those whose safety or national goals depend on American commitments could only be dismayed. In many parts of the world—the Middle East, Europe, Latin America, even Japan—stability depends on confidence in American promises. Unilateral withdrawal or a settlement which, even unintentionally, amounts to it could therefore lead to the erosion of restraints and to an even more dangerous international situation.

Hanoi's position is at least as complicated. Its concerns are not global; they are xenophobically Vietnamese (which includes, of course, hegemonic ambitions in Laos and Cambodia). But Hanoi is extraordinarily dependent on the international environment. It could not continue the war without foreign material assistance. It counts almost as heavily on the pressures of world public opinion. Any event that detracts from global preoccupations with the war in Vietnam thus diminishes Hanoi's bargaining position. From this point of view, the Soviet invasion of Czechoslovakia was a major setback for Hanoi.

Hanoi's margin of survival is so narrow that precise calculation has become a way of life; caution is almost an obsession. Its bargaining position depends on a fine assessment of international factors—especially of the jungle of intra-Communist relations. In order to retain its autonomy, Hanoi must maneuver skillfully between Peking, Moscow, and the NLF. Hanoi has no desire to become completely dependent on one of the Communist giants. But, since they disagree violently, they reinforce Hanoi's already strong tendency toward obscurantist formulations. In short, Hanoi's freedom to maneuver is severely limited.

The same is true of the Soviet Union, whose large-scale aid to Hanoi makes it a semi-participant in the war. Moscow must be torn by contradictory emotions. A complete victory for Hanoi would tend to benefit Peking in the struggle for influence in the world Communist parties: it would support the Chinese argument that intransigence toward the United States is, if not without risk, at least relatively manageable. But a defeat of Hanoi would demonstrate Soviet inability to protect "fraternal" Communist countries against the United States. It would also weaken a potential barrier to Chinese influence in Southeast Asia, and enable Peking to turn its full fury on Moscow. For a long time, Moscow has seemed paralyzed by conflicting considerations and bureaucratic inertia.

Events in Czechoslovakia have reduced Moscow's usefulness even further. Any attempt by Moscow to settle the war would add fuel to the already widespread charge that the superpowers are sacrificing their allies to maintain spheres of influence. Washington therefore requires great delicacy in dealing with Moscow over Vietnam. We would compound the heavy costs of our pallid reaction to events in Czechoslovakia if our allies could blame it on a *quid pro quo* for Soviet assistance in extricating us from Southeast Asia.

This state of affairs would be enough to explain prolonged negotiations progressing through a series of stalemates. In addition, a vast gulf in cultural and bureaucratic style between Hanoi and Washington complicates matters further. It would be difficult to imagine two societies less meant to understand each other than the Vietnamese and the American. History and culture combine to produce almost morbid suspiciousness on the part of the Vietnamese. Because survival has depended on a subtle skill in manipulating physically stronger foreigners, the Vietnamese style of communication is indirect and, by American standards, devious—qualities which avoid a total commitment and an overt test of strength. The fear of being made to look foolish seems to transcend most other considerations. Even if the United States accepted Hanoi's maximum program, the result might well be months of haggling while Hanoi looks for our "angle," and makes sure that no other concessions are likely to be forthcoming.

These tendencies are magnified by Communist ideology which defines the United States as structurally hostile and by Hanoi's experience in previous negotiations with the United States. It may well feel that the Geneva Conferences of 1954

and 1962 (over Laos) deprived it of part of its achievements
on the battlefield.

All this produces the particular negotiating style of Hanoi:
the careful planning, the subtle, indirect methods, the pref-
erence for opaque communications which keep open as many
options as possible toward both foe and friend (the latter may
be equally important from Hanoi's point of view). Hanoi's
diplomacy operates in phases of reconnaissance and withdrawal to give an opportunity to assess the opponent's reaction. This is then followed by another diplomatic sortie to
consolidate the achievements of the previous phase or to try
another route. In this sense, many contacts with Hanoi which
seemed "abortive" to us probably served the function of defining the terrain from Hanoi's point of view. The methods
of Hanoi's diplomacy are not very different from Viet Cong
military strategy and sometimes appear just as impenetrable
to us.

If this analysis is correct, few moves by Hanoi are acci-
dental; even the most obtuse communication is likely to serve
a purpose. On the other hand, it is not a style which easily
reveals itself to the sort of analysis at which we excel: the
pragmatic, legal dissection of individual cases. Where Hanoi
makes a fetish of planning, Washington is allergic to it. It
prefers to deal with cases as they arise, "on their merits." Pronouncements that the United States is ready to negotiate do
not guarantee that a negotiating position exists or that the
United States government has articulated its objectives.

Until a conference comes to be scheduled, two groups in the
American bureaucracy usually combine to thwart the elaboration of a negotiating position: those who oppose negotiations
and those who favor them. The opponents generally equate
negotiations with surrender; if they agree to discuss settlement terms at all it is to define the conditions of the enemy's

capitulation. Aware of this tendency and of the reluctance of the top echelon to expend capital on settling disputes which involve no immediate practical consequences, the advocates of negotiations cooperate in avoiding the issue. Moreover, since they generally have great confidence in their negotiating skill, delay serves their own bureaucratic purposes: it enables them to reserve freedom of action for the conference room.

Pragmatism and bureaucracy thus combine to produce the American diplomatic style of rigidity before formal negotiations and of excessive reliance on tactical considerations once negotiations start. In the preliminary phases, we generally lack a negotiating program; during the conference, bargaining considerations tend to shape internal discussions. In the process, we deprive ourselves of criteria by which to judge progress. The overconcern with tactics suppresses a feeling for nuance and for intangibles.

The incompatibility of the American and North Vietnamese style of diplomacy produced, for a long time, a massive breakdown of communication—especially in the preliminary phases of negotiations. While Hanoi was feeling its way toward negotiations, it bent all its ingenuity to avoid clear-cut, formal commitments. Ambiguity permitted Hanoi to probe without giving away anything in return; Hanoi has no peers in slicing the salami very thin. It wanted the context of events to define its obligations rather than a formal document which might compromise it with Peking or the NLF.

Washington was unequipped for this mode of communication. To a government identifying commitments with legally enforceable obligations, Hanoi's subtle changes of tense were literally incomprehensible. In a press conference in February 1968, President Johnson said, "As near as I am able to detect, Hanoi has not changed its course of conduct since the very first response it made. Sometimes they will change 'will' to 'would' or 'shall' to 'should,' or something of the kind. But the answer is all the same." [3] A different kind of analysis might have inquired why Hanoi would open up a channel for a meaningless communication, especially in the light of a record of careful planning which made it extremely unlikely that a change of tense would be inadvertent.

Whatever the might-have-beens, Hanoi appeared to Washington as devious, deceitful, and tricky. To Hanoi, Washington must have seemed, if not obtuse, then cannily purposeful. In any event, the deadlock produced by the difference in negotiating style concerned less specific clauses than the philosophical issue of the nature of an international "commitment" or the meaning of "trickery." This problem lay at the heart of the recently broken impasse over the bombing halt.

3. *New York Times*, February 17, 1968.

III. COMMITMENT AND RISK IN VIETNAM DIPLOMACY: THE PROBLEM OF THE BOMBING HALT

THE BOMBING HALT occupied the first six months of the Paris talks. The formal positions were relatively straightforward. The American view was encompassed in the so-called San Antonio formula which was put forth by President Johnson in September 1967: "The United States is willing to stop all aerial and naval bombardment of North Vietnam when this will lead promptly to productive discussions. We, of course, assume that while discussions proceed, North Vietnam would not take advantage of the bombing cessation or limitation." [4] In its main outlines, the American position remained unchanged throughout the negotiations.

Hanoi's reaction was equally simple and stark. It scored the obvious debating point that it could guarantee useful but not "productive" talks since that depended also on the United States. [5] But in the main, Hanoi adamantly insisted that the bombing halt had to be "unconditional." It rejected all American proposals for reciprocity as put forward for example by Secretary Rusk: respect for the DMZ, no attack on South

4. *New York Times,* September 30, 1967.
5. Article by Wilfred Burchett, *New York Times,* October 21, 1967.

Vietnamese cities, reduction in the level of military operations.[6]

Though this deadlock had many causes, surely a central problem was the difficulty each side had in articulating its real concern. Washington feared "trickery"; it believed that once stopped, the bombing would be difficult, if not impossible, to start again even in the face of considerable provocation. Too, it needed some assurance as to how the negotiations would proceed *after* a bombing halt. Washington was aware that a bombing halt which did not lead rapidly to substantive talks could not be sustained domestically.

The legalistic phrasing of these concerns obscured their real merit. If bombing were resumed under conditions of great public indignation, it would be much harder to exercise restraint in the choice of targets and much more difficult to stop again in order to test Hanoi's intentions. The frequently heard advice to "take risks for peace" is valid only if one is aware that the consequence of an imprudent risk is likely to be escalation rather than peace.

Hanoi, in turn, had a special reason for insisting on an unconditional end of the bombing. A government as subtle as Hanoi must have known that there are no "unconditional" acts in the relations of sovereign states, if only because sovereignty implies the right to reassess changing conditions unilaterally. But Hanoi has always placed great reliance on the pressures of world opinion; the "illegality" of the United States bombing was therefore a potent political weapon. Reciprocity would jeopardize this claim; it suggested that the United States bombing might be justified in some circumstances. Hanoi did not want a formula under which the United States could resume bombing "legally" by charging

6. See Secretary Rusk on "Issues & Answers," October 6, 1968.

violations of an understanding. Finally, Hanoi was eager to give the impression to its supporters in the South that it had induced us to stop "unconditionally" as a symbol of imminent victory. For the same reason, it was important to us that *both* sides in South Vietnam believed there had been reciprocity.

As a result, six months were devoted to defining a *quid pro quo* which could be represented as unconditional. The issue of the bombing halt thus raised the question of the nature of an international commitment. What is the sanction for violation of an understanding? The United States, for a long time, conducted itself as if its principal safeguard was a formal, binding commitment by Hanoi to certain restraints. In fact, since no court exists to which the United States could take Hanoi, the American sanction is what the United States can do unilaterally should Hanoi "take advantage" of the bombing pause. Hanoi's fear of the consequences is a more certain protection against trickery than a formal commitment. Communicating what we meant by taking advantage turned out to be more important than eliciting a formal North Vietnamese response.

The final settlement of the problem seems to have been arrived at by this procedure. In his address announcing the bombing halt, President Johnson stressed that Hanoi is clear about our definition of "take advantage." Hanoi has not formally acknowledged these terms; it has, in fact, insisted that the bombing halt was unconditional. But Hanoi can have little doubt that the bombing halt would not survive an escalation of the war in the categories publicly stated by Secretary Rusk.

If the negotiations about the bombing halt demonstrate that tacit bargaining may play a crucial role in an ultimate settlement, they also show the extraordinary danger of neglecting the political framework. Washington had insisted throughout the negotiations that Saigon participate in the substantive talks which were to follow a bombing halt. President Johnson, in his speech announcing the bombing halt, implied that Saigon's participation satisfied the requirement of the San Antonio formula for "productive talks." How we came to insist on a condition which was basically neither in our interest nor in Saigon's cannot be determined until the records are available—if then. It should have been clear that the participation of Saigon was bound to raise the issues of the status of the NLF and the internal structure of Vietnam— issues which, as will be seen below, it is in everybody's interest to defer to as late a stage of the negotiations as possible.

Having made Saigon's participation a test case, we advanced the "your side, our side" formula. Under it, Saigon and the NLF are to participate in the conference. Each side can claim that it is composed of two delegations; its opponent is free to insist that it really deals with only one delegation. Thus the United States does not "recognize" the NLF and insists that Hanoi is its negotiating partner; Hanoi can take the opposite view and maintain its refusal to deal formally with Saigon. It is difficult to disentangle from public sources whether Saigon ever agreed to this formula or whether it understood that our formula amounted to giving the NLF equal status.[7] On the face of it, Saigon's reluc-

7. Clashes with our allies in which both sides claim to have been deceived happen so frequently as to suggest structural causes (see Skybolt, the nonproliferation treaty, now the bombing halt). What seems to be happening is the same bureaucratic deadlock internationally which was noted above within our government. When an issue is fairly abstract —before there is a prospect for an agreement—our diplomats tend to present our view in a bland, relaxed fashion to the ally whose interests are involved but who is not present at the negotiations. The ally responds equally vaguely for three reasons: (a) he may be misled into believing that no decision is imminent and therefore sees no purpose in making an issue; (b) he is afraid that if he forces the issue the decision will go against him; (c) he hopes the problem will go away because agreement

tance to accept equal status with the NLF is comprehensible, for it tends to affect all other issues from ceasefire to internal structure. The merits of the dispute aside, the public rift between Saigon and Washington compromised what had been achieved. To split Washington and Saigon has been a constant objective of Hanoi; if the Paris talks turn into an instrument to accomplish this, Hanoi will be tempted to use them for political warfare rather than for serious discussions.

Clearly, there is a point beyond which Saigon cannot be given a veto over negotiations. But equally, it is not preposterous for Saigon to insist on a major voice over decisions affecting its own country. And it cannot strengthen our position in Paris to *begin* the substantive discussions with a public row over the status of the government whose constitutional origin we insistently pressed on the world for the past two years. The impasse—which will no doubt be broken sooner or later—demonstrates that to deal with issues on an *ad hoc* basis is too risky; before we go much further in negotiations, we need an agreed concept of ultimate goals and how to achieve them.

---

will prove impossible. When agreement seems imminent, American diplomats suddenly go into high gear to gain the acquiescence of the ally. He in turn feels tricked by the very intensity and suddenness of the pressure while we are outraged to learn of objections heretofore not made explicit. This almost guarantees that the ensuing controversy will take place under the most difficult conditions.

IV. CEASEFIRE AND
COALITION GOVERNMENT

SUBSTANTIVE negotiations confront the United States with a major conceptual problem: whether to proceed step by step, discussing each item "on its merits," or whether to begin by attempting to get agreement about some ultimate goals.

The difference is not trivial. If the negotiations proceed step by step through a formal agenda, the danger is great that the bombing halt will turn out to be an admission ticket to another deadlock. The issues are so interrelated that a partial settlement foreshadows the ultimate outcome and therefore contains all of its complexities. Mutual distrust and the absence of clarity as to final goals combine to produce an extraordinary incentive to submit all proposals to the most searching scrutiny and to erect hedges for failure or bad faith.

This is well illustrated by two schemes which public debate has identified as suitable topics for the next stage of negotiations: ceasefire and coalition government.

It has become axiomatic that a bombing halt would lead —almost automatically—to a ceasefire. However, negotiating a ceasefire may well be tantamount to establishing the preconditions of a political settlement. If there existed a front line with unchallenged control behind it as in Korea, the solution would be traditional and relatively simple: the two sides could stop shooting at each other and the ceasefire line could follow the front line. But there are no front lines in Vietnam; control is not territorial, it depends on who has forces in a given area and on the time of day. If a ceasefire permits the government to move without challenge, day or night, it would define a Saigon victory. If Saigon is prevented from entering certain areas, it would mean in effect partition which, as in Laos, would tend toward permanency. Unlike Laos, however, the pattern would be a crazy quilt with enclaves of conflicting loyalties all over the country.

This would involve the following additional problems: (a) it would lead to an intense scramble to establish predominant control before the ceasefire goes into effect; (b) it would make next to impossible the verification of any withdrawal of North Vietnamese forces that might be negotiated; the local authorities in areas of preponderant Communist control would doubtless certify that no external forces were present and impede any effort at international inspection; (c) it would raise the problem of the applicability of a ceasefire to guerrilla activity in the non-Communist part of the country; in other words, how to deal with the asymmetry between the actions of regular and of guerrilla forces. Regular forces operate on a scale which makes possible a relatively precise definition of what is permitted and what is proscribed; guerrilla forces, by contrast, can be effective through isolated acts of terror difficult to distinguish from normal criminal activity.

There are many other problems in the typical cases of dual control: who collects taxes and how, who enforces the ceasefire and by what means. In other words, a tacit *de facto* ceasefire may prove more attainable than a negotiated one. By the same token, a formal ceasefire is likely to predetermine the ultimate settlement and tend toward partition. Ceasefire is thus not so much a step toward a final settlement as a form of it.

This is even more true of another staple of the Vietnam debate: the notion of a coalition government. Of course, there are two meanings of the term: (a) as a means of legitimizing partition, indeed as a disguise for continuing the civil war, (b) as a "true" coalition government attempting to govern the whole country. In the first case, a coalition government would be a facade with non-Communist and Communist ministries in effect governing their own part of the country. This is what happened in Laos, where each party in the "coalition government" wound up with its own armed forces and its own territorial administration. The central government did not exercise any truly national functions. Each side carried on its own business—including civil war. But in Laos, each side controlled contiguous territory, not a series of enclaves as in South Vietnam. Furthermore, of all the ways to bring about partition, negotiations about a coalition government are the most dangerous because the mere participation of the United States in talking about it could change the political landscape of South Vietnam.

Coalition government is perhaps the most emotionally charged issue in Vietnam, where it tends to be identified with the second meaning: a joint Saigon-NLF administration of the entire country. There can be no American objection, of course, to direct negotiations between Saigon and the NLF. The issue is whether the United States should be party to an attempt to *impose* a coalition government. We must be clear that our involvement in such an effort may well destroy the existing political structure of South Vietnam and thus lead to a Communist takeover.

Some urge negotiations on a coalition government for precisely this reason: as a face-saving formula for arranging the Communist political victory which they consider inevitable. But those who believe that the political evolution of South Vietnam should not be foreclosed by an American decision must realize that the subject of a coalition government is the most thankless and tricky area for negotiation *by outsiders.*

The notion that a coalition government represents a "compromise" which will permit a new political evolution hardly does justice to Vietnamese conditions. To "solve" the problems of Vietnam by means of a coalition government makes as much sense as to attempt to overcome the problems of Mississippi through a coalition between the SDS and the Ku Klux Klan. Even the non-Communist groups have demonstrated the difficulty Vietnamese have in compromising differences. It is beyond imagination that parties that have been murdering and betraying each other for twenty-five years could work together as a team giving joint instructions to the entire country. The image of a line of command extending from Saigon into the countryside is hardly true of the non-Communist government in Saigon. It would be absurd in the case of a coalition government. Such a government would possess no authority other than that of each minister over the forces he controls through either personal or party loyalty.

To take just one example of the difficulties: Communist ministers would be foolhardy in the extreme if they entered Saigon without bringing along sufficient military force for their protection. But the introduction of Communist military forces into the chief bastion of governmental strength would change the balance of political forces in South Vietnam. The danger of a coalition government is that it would decouple the non-Communist elements from effective control over their armed forces and police, leaving them unable to defend themselves adequately.

In short, negotiations seeking to impose a coalition from the outside are likely to change markedly and irreversibly the political process in South Vietnam as Vietnamese who believe that a coalition government cannot work quickly choose sides. We would, in effect, be settling the war over the issue least amenable to outside influence, with respect to which we have the least grasp of conditions, and the long-term implications of which are most problematical.

This is not to say that the United States should resist a coalition government if it came about freely through negotiations between the Vietnamese, especially in the first sense of legitimizing separate administrations—in that case, in fact, the United States would be in no position to resist. It does suggest that any negotiation about it by the United States is likely to lead either to an impasse or to the collapse of Saigon.

V. WHERE DO WE GO
FROM HERE?

PARADOXICAL as it may seem, the best way to make progress where distrust is so deep and the issues so interrelated may be to seek agreement on ultimate goals first and to work back to the details to implement it.

This requires an analysis of the strengths and weaknesses of both sides. Hanoi's strength is that it is fighting among its own people in familiar territory, while the United States is fighting far away. As long as Hanoi can preserve some political assets in the South, it retains the prospect of an ultimately favorable political outcome. Not surprisingly, Hanoi has shown a superior grasp of the local situation and a greater capacity to design military operations for political ends. Hanoi relies on world opinion and American domestic pressures; it believes that the unpopularity of the war in Vietnam will ultimately force an American withdrawal.

Hanoi's weaknesses are that superior planning can substitute for material resources only up to a point. Beyond it, differences of scale are bound to become significant and a continuation of the war will require a degree of foreign assistance which may threaten Hanoi's autonomy. This Hanoi has jealously guarded until now. A prolonged, even if ultimately victorious, war might leave Vietnam so exhausted as to jeopardize the purpose of decades of struggles.

Moreover, a country as sensitive to international currents as North Vietnam cannot be reassured by recent developments. The Soviet invasion of Czechoslovakia removed Vietnam as the principal concern of world opinion at least for a while. Some countries heretofore critical of the United States remembered their own peril and their need for the United States' protection; this served to reduce the intensity of public pressures on America. Hanoi's support of Moscow demonstrated the degree of Hanoi's dependence on the U.S.S.R. It also may have been intended to forestall Soviet pressures on Hanoi to be more flexible by putting Moscow in Hanoi's debt. Whatever the reason, the vision of a Titoist Vietnam suddenly seemed less plausible—all the more so as Moscow's justification for the invasion of Czechoslovakia can provide a theoretical basis for an eventual Chinese move against North Vietnam. Finally, the Soviet doctrine according to which Moscow has a right to intervene to protect Socialist domestic structures made a Sino-Soviet war at least conceivable, for Moscow's accusations against Peking have been, if anything, even sharper than those against Prague. But in case of a Sino-Soviet conflict, Hanoi would be left high and dry. Thus, Hanoi may, for the first time, feel that time is not necessarily on its side.

American assets and liabilities are the reverse of this. No matter how irrelevant some of our political conceptions or how insensitive our strategy, we are so powerful that Hanoi is simply unable to defeat us militarily. By its own efforts, Hanoi cannot force the withdrawal of American forces from South Vietnam. Indeed, a substantial improvement in the American military position seems to have taken place. As a result, we have achieved our minimum objective: Hanoi is unable to gain a military victory. Since it cannot force our withdrawal, it must negotiate about it. Unfortunately, our military strength has no political corollary; we have been unable so far to create a political structure that could survive military opposition from Hanoi after we withdraw.

The structure of the negotiation is thus quite different from Korea. There are no front lines with secure areas behind them. In Vietnam, negotiations do not ratify a military status quo but create a new political reality. There are no unambiguous tests of relative political and military strength. The political situation for both sides is precarious—within Vietnam for the United States, internationally for Hanoi. Thus it is probable that neither side can risk a negotiation so prolonged as that of Panmunjom a decade and a half ago. In such a situation, a favorable outcome depends on a clear definition of objectives. The limits of the American commitment can be expressed in two propositions: (a) the United States cannot accept a military defeat, or a change in the political structure of South Vietnam brought about by external military force; (b) once North Vietnamese forces and pressures are removed, the United States has no obligation to maintain a government in Saigon by force.

American objectives should therefore be to (a) bring about a staged withdrawal of external forces, North Vietnamese and American, (b) thereby to create a maximum incentive for the contending forces in South Vietnam to work out a political agreement. The structure and content of such an agreement must be left to the South Vietnamese. It could take place formally on the national level. Or, it could occur locally on the provincial level, where even now tacit accommodations are not unusual in many areas such as the Mekong Delta.

The details of a phased, mutual withdrawal are not decisive for our present purposes and, in any case, would have to be left to negotiations. It is possible, however, to list some principles: (a) the withdrawal should be over a sufficiently long period so that a genuine indigenous political process has a chance to become established; mutual withdrawal cannot be treated as a camouflage for a Communist takeover; (b) the contending sides in South Vietnam should commit themselves not to pursue their objectives by force while the withdrawal of external forces is going on; (c) insofar as possible, the definition of what constitutes a suitable political process or structure should be left to the South Vietnamese, with the mutual withdrawal creating the time frame for an agreement.

This analysis suggests the thrust for American policy in the next phase: the United States should concentrate on the subject of the mutual withdrawal of external forces and avoid negotiating about the internal structure of South Vietnam for as long as possible. The primary responsibility for negotiating the internal structure of South Vietnam should be left for direct negotiations among the South Vietnamese. If we involve ourselves deeply in the issue of South Vietnam's internal arrangements, we will find ourselves in a morass of complexities subject to two major disadvantages: (a) we would be the party in the negotiation least attuned to the subtleties of Vietnamese politics; (b) our pressure may wind up being directed against Saigon as the seeming obstacle to an accommodation. The result may be the complete demoralization of Saigon, profound domestic tensions within the United States, and a prolonged stalemate or a resumption of the war.

In such an approach, the negotiating procedure becomes vital; indeed, it may well determine the outcome and the speed with which it is achieved.

Tying the bombing halt to Saigon's participation in the substantive discussions was probably unwise—all the more so as Hanoi seems to have been prepared to continue bilateral talks. The participation of Saigon and the NLF raised issues about status that would have been better deferred; it made a discussion of the internal structure of South Vietnam hard to avoid. Nevertheless, the principles sketched above, while now more difficult to implement, can still guide the negotiations. The tension between Washington and Saigon can even prove salutary if it forces both sides to learn that if they are to negotiate effectively they must confront the fundamental issues explicitly.

As these lines are being written, the formula for resolving the issue of Saigon's participation in the conference is not yet clear. But the general approach should be the same whatever the eventual compromise.

The best procedure would be to establish three forums. If the South Vietnamese finally appear in Paris—as is probable —the four-sided conference should be primarily a plenary legitimizing session for two subcommittees which need not be formally established and could even meet secretly: (a) between Hanoi and the United States, and (b) between Saigon and the NLF. Hanoi and Washington would discuss mutual troop withdrawal and related subjects such as guarantees for the neutrality of Laos and Cambodia. Saigon and the NLF would discuss the internal structure of South Vietnam. The third forum would be an international conference to work out guarantees and safeguards for the agreements arrived at in the other forums, including international peacekeeping machinery.

If Saigon continues to refuse the "our side, your side" formula, the same procedure could be followed. The subcommittees would become principal forums and the four-sided plenary session would be eliminated. The international "guaranteeing conference" would not be affected.

To be sure, Saigon, for understandable reasons, has consistently refused to deal with the NLF as an international entity. But if Saigon understands its own interests, it will come to realize that the procedure outlined here involves a minimum and necessary concession. The three-tiered approach gives Saigon the greatest possible control over the issues that affect its own fate; direct negotiations between the United States and the NLF would be obviated. A sovereign government is free to talk to any group that represents an important power base domestically without thereby conferring sovereignty on it; it happens domestically all the time in union negotiations or even in police work.

But why should Hanoi accept such an approach? The answer is that partly it has no choice; it cannot bring about a withdrawal of American forces by its own efforts—particularly if the United States adopts a less impatient strategy, geared to the protection of the population and sustainable with substantially reduced casualties. Hanoi may also believe that, being better organized and more determined, the NLF can win a political contest. (Of course, the prerequisite of a settlement is that both sides think they have a chance to win or at least to avoid losing.) Above all, Hanoi may not wish to give the United States a permanent voice in internal South Vietnamese affairs, as it would if the conference emerging from the "our side, your side" formula becomes the sole forum. It may be reinforced in this attitude by the belief that a prolonged negotiation about coalition government may end no more satisfactorily from Hanoi's point of view than the Geneva negotiations over Vietnam in 1954 and Laos in 1962. As for the United States, if it brings about a removal of external forces and pressure, and if it gains a reasonable time for political consolidation, it will have done the maximum possible for an ally—short of permanent occupation.

To be sure, Hanoi cannot be asked to leave the NLF to the mercy of Saigon. While a coalition government is undesirable, a mixed commission to develop and supervise a political process to reintegrate the country—including free elections—could be useful. And there must be an international presence to enforce good faith. Similarly, we cannot be expected to rely on Hanoi's word that the removal of its forces and pressures from South Vietnam is permanent. An international force would be required to supervise access routes. It should be reinforced by an electronic barrier to check movements.

A negotiating procedure and a definition of objectives cannot guarantee a settlement, of course. If Hanoi insists on total victory, the war must continue. Any other posture would destroy the chances of a settlement and encourage Hanoi to wait us out. In that case, we should seek to achieve as many of our objectives as possible unilaterally. We should adopt a strategy which is plausible because it reduces casualties. It should concentrate on the protection of the population, thereby undermining Communist political assets. We should continue to strengthen the Vietnamese army to permit a gradual withdrawal of some American forces. Saigon should broaden its base so that it is stronger for the political contest with the Communists which sooner or later it must undertake.

No war in a century has aroused the passions of the conflict in Vietnam. By turning Vietnam into a symbol of deeper resentments, many groups have defeated the objective they profess to seek. However we got into Vietnam, whatever the judgment of our actions, ending the war honorably is essential for the peace of the world. Any other solution may unloose forces that would complicate prospects of international order. A new administration must be given the benefit of the doubt and a chance to move toward a peace which grants the people of Vietnam what they have struggled so bravely to achieve: an opportunity to work out their own destiny in their own way.

INDEX

Bureaucracy *(cont.)*
 negotiating positions thwarted
  by, 115–16
 pervasiveness of modern, 94–95
 placating, 20–21
 purpose of, 18
 Soviet, 21, 87
 of state, 94–97
 vested interests of, 17
 See also Leadership
Bureaucratic-pragmatic leadership,
 29–34
 American élite as, 29
 concerned with symptoms, 32–33
 constitutional solutions as bias of,
  34
 decision-making as bargaining
  process of, 30–31
 historical factors for, 33–34
 rejection of, 39
 segmentation of problems by, 29–
  30
Bureaucratization, rationality and,
 46
Burke, Edmund, 12–13
Business élite, characterized, 32; *see
 also* Bureaucratic-pragmatic
 leadership

Calculability, arbitrary decisions
 and, 23
Cambodia, 113
 neutralization of, 132
Castro, F., 86
 motivation of, 39, 40
Ceasefire
 in Korea, 124
 in Vietnam, 123–25
CENTO (Central Treaty Organization), 66–67
Charismatic-revolutionary leadership, 39–43
 motivation of, 39–40
 reckless policy of, 40–42
China
 influence of, in Africa, 42
 invasion of Czechoslovakia and,
  129
 nuclear weapons and, 60
 policy changes in, 38–39
 Sino-Soviet dispute, 36, 37–38
 special problem in dealing with,
  91
 Vietnam war and, 113–14
Class struggle, 35–37, 79

Coalition government in Vietnam,
 125–27
Commitments, multiplication of, 92;
 see also Vietnam war
Common Market, 74
Communism, legitimacy through,
 34–35, 83; *see also* Marxism;
 Marxism-Leninism
Communist parties, 87
Congress of Vienna, 48
Conjecture, 14
Consensus in Imperial Germany,
 27–28
Consultation, limitations of, 72–74
Containment, original purpose of,
 86
Cooperation, basis for U.S.-Euro-
 pean, 71–72, 74–78
 areas for cooperation, 77–78
Coordination, 76
Crises
 in NATO, 70
 order and, 49–50; *see also* Order
 twentieth-century, 52
Czechoslovakia, occupation of (1968),
 55, 88
 China and, 129
 effect on Vietnam war of, 113,
  114, 129
 implications of, 89
 as limit to autonomy, 77
 NATO countries and, 67
 U.S. response, 70

Decision-making
 as bargaining process of bureaucratic-pragmatic leadership,
  30–31
 bureaucratic, 17–26
  alliances and, 24
  executive as arbiter, 22–23
  institutionalization of process,
   17
  presenting facts, 21–22
  random, 25–26
  rigidity of process, 19–20
Decisions
 calculability and arbitrary, 23
 delimiting nature of, 45
 margin of, 13–14
Democracy
 nationalism and, 82
 presupposition of, 41
Détente, 88–90

Underdeveloped countries, *see* Developing nations
United States
  alliance system of, 66–67; *see also* Alliances
  concentration on relations with Soviet Union, 78
  concept of international cooperation and, 74–75
  as conscious creation, 79–80
  diplomacy of, 31; *see also* Diplomacy
  Europe and, 67–72, 74–78
    areas for cooperation, 77–78
    basis for cooperation, 71–72, 74–76
    European recovery and U.S. ascendancy, 68–69
    NATO, *see* NATO
    reversal of roles, 67–68
  negotiating qualities of, 31–32; *see also* Negotiations
  Pueblo capture and, 63
  reliance of, on economic factors, 84
  response to invasion of Czechoslovakia, 70
  role of, in building legitimacy, 82
  world order and, 57
  See also Bureaucratic-pragmatic leadership; National interest; Vietnam negotiations; Vietnam war
Unrest, 96–97
U.S.S.R., *see* Soviet Union

Vietnam, North and South, *see* Vietnam negotiations; Vietnam war
Vietnam negotiations, 100–35
  best procedure for, 132–34
  bombing halt in, 118–22
    Johnson's San Antonio formula, 118
    reciprocity proposals, 118–20
  complicated positions in, 112–14
  conditions for seeking, 106–8
  contacts prior to, 109–10
  events leading to, 101
  freedom of action in, 110–11
  goals in, 123–27
    ceasefire, 123–25
    coalition government, 125–27

specific goals, 130–31
  negotiating styles in, 114–17
  negotiating positions, 31
  wariness in, 111–12
  weakness and strengths in, 128–30
  "your side, our side" formula in, 121–22
Vietnam war
  breakdown in communication and, 63
  China and, 113–14
  dual-control in, 104
  escalation of, 33
  guerrilla strategy in, 102, 104
  as introduction to politics, 95
  Johnson's policy in, 63
    bombing halted, 120, 121
    Johnson's San Antonio formula, 118
    negotiation offers, 105
    on negotiation style of North Vietnamese, 116–17
    quest for settlement (Mar. 1968), 108
    view of pacification, 101
  legacy of, 97
  military strategy in, 101–5
  notion of security in, 103
  pacification program in, 105–6
    Johnson's view of program, 101
  as precedent, 62
  realistic appraisal of, 103–4
  Soviet Union and, 113–14
  Tet offensive in (1968), 101, 106–8
  See also Vietnam negotiations

War
  guerrilla, 102–4
  of kings, 13
  See also Military bipolarity; Nuclear war

Warsaw Pact, 76
West, view of reality in, 48–49
West European Union (WEU), 76
Western Europe, 91
  defense of, 71
  Eastern and, 78
  Soviet nuclear power and, 60
Westernization, global, 44
Westmoreland, General W., 101
World order, *see* Order

Youth, 95–97

Zhukov, Marshal G., 37

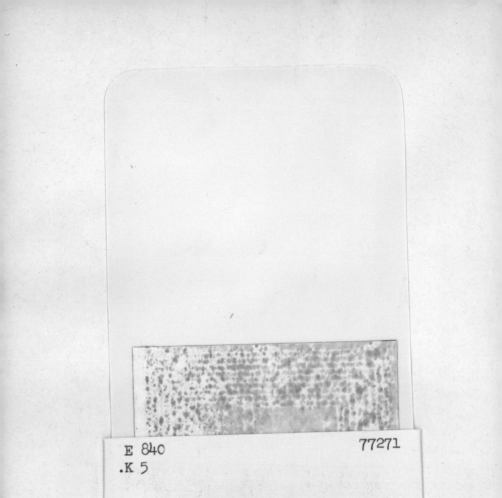